MAN

Created

GOD

BY

CARL L CROZIER

Man Created God

Carl L. Crozier

ISBN-13: 978-0-9977051-9-5

Library of Congress Control Number: 2019905240

Copyright © 2019 Carl L. Crozier

carlcrozier10@gmail.com

Printed in the United States of America.

BELLA JOHNS ENTERPRISES
PUBLISHER

Introduction

There have been many gods celebrated by man since man's existence on Earth and since man began to fear the unknown. Zeus, Poseidon, Thor, Yahweh, Wen and Christ are only a few of the thousands of gods that man has named and honored. Early man, using his imagination and creativity, created a god for every earthly phenomenon that affected their lives. There was a god for fire, water, love and war etc. Later in the history of man, man deemed those early gods that had been invented by man as pagan gods and the people that worshipped them pagans. Being deemed a pagan was not a term of endearment.

At a certain period in the life of mankind, man shifted from the theory of multiple gods to the theory that there was (is) only one god who controls the behavior of the earth and man. Again, man used his imagination and creativity to come up with a concept of a god more in line with the thinking of a more intelligent species.

Men could not agree on the name of the one god or who the one god was. Many times, man fought bloody wars over what god was going to be recognized as the one true god. The Christians and the Muslims killed each other for centuries to try and determine whether the true god was going to be Christ or Allah. Their religious wars were never decisive in that the proponents never settled on who the one god would be. To this day both groups, Christians and Muslims, still have their individual god.

Other religious groups around the world also have an individual god who they worship and adore. The Buddhists, Hindus, Confucians and other religious groups have their god and they try to sell their god as the one true god.

This book examines the myth of god and attempts to explain that man created god to try to fill the void of knowledge with the concept of faith in a supernatural being who was capable of doing all things that effected man because man lacked understanding of how the world worked but did not want to live in a godless world.

This is a book about my perception of God and Religion. I am an atheist. I don't believe in God.

God is a man-made creation. God was created by man because there are so many things in the existence of man and his surroundings that man does not understand and could not explain. Thus, man created God to be responsible for the things that man did not comprehend about life. In looking for answers to solve life's questions man found it comforting to invent god.

I'm not claiming to be a religious scholar. I am just an inquiring mind who can and is allowed to ask some common-sense questions about religion and about the deity called God.

Many people claim to be religious scholars. They have studied at universities and have earned various degrees when their studies were concluded. Part of their education has been involved with the study of other men who have studied religion. Those that have studied religion early in history have been given the title Theologian. A Theologian is a specialist in Theology. Theology is the study of God and the relationship between God and the universe. Those learned men who have spent many years of study postulate that they know God and they are aware of god's intent. They write books, preach sermons and dictate to their followers that they have an understanding in matters that relate to God and that their followers should have faith in the existence of a god that has been explained to them.

The Pope, the Imam, and religious leaders of Hinduism, Buddhism and all other religions in the world indicate they have a unique relationship with god. Store front preachers, street corner healers, cult leaders and television evangelists have all taken up the mantra that they know God and are privy to what God wants us to do.

People who believe in the same god have evoked god's name in the furtherance of their religious cause. Europe is a mostly Christian area of the world. That continent is divided into a number of different countries that from time to time, throughout history have warred with each other. They all believe in, pray to and indicate to their countrymen that god is on their side.

World War I (1914–1918) was not fought about God but most of the European countries that were involved were Christian countries and they all prayed to the Christian God when they went off to war. They went off to battle after being blessed by "Gods representative" before they went to fight. England and France won the war and Germany was left to crawl in the dirt of defeat. All those countries had faith that God would take them to victory, but it appeared the Germans blind subservience to an imaginary being didn't pay off. More than 5 million men died because both sides thought that their cause was righteous in the eyes of God.

There have been wars where the object of the war was to determine which god or religion would govern the populous – Christian vs Muslin is one such war (The crusades around the 10th and the 11th centuries). It doesn't matter what the differences are between the tenets of each religion but a lot of men who didn't know the differences between the religions died – led by so called holy men who professed to know the differences between their deities.

History tells us that people need to believe in something and men will go to their death because they have faith in their religious beliefs. There are many religions and many religious beliefs throughout the world. You are told that you do not have to have an experience to have religious faith. Religious faith does not require that you understand what you believe in. Faith alone will sustain you in a religion, so you are told by the purveyors of the creed. Experience is not required.

I have faith in my car getting from one place to another because I have experienced the car going that distance before. I beat cancer because I had faith in modern medicine because I knew that other people had successful experiences using the drugs that saved my life.

I have met people who said that they had an experience with God. I ask them, "can I duplicate your experience?" They say "no". They say that Jesus Christ, the son of God, walked on water. Can his experience be duplicated? "No" they answer. The Wright brothers said that they built and flew a machine that could fly. Other men had faith that flying could be accomplished and they were able to duplicate the brother's experience. New ideas are discovered throughout history and those ideas are tested. If the ideas become a proven reality, they become authentic and are counted as a realism that can be relied upon to occur again and again under the same given circumstances. Religious faith is defined as a belief without true understanding; it's not based on logic. Most of religions is (was) based on supposition, imagination or myth. Modern science has already disproved much that was in the Bible that went for fact in religious philosophy.

Most people believe in life after death. For those that believe in that concept, I wonder what they envision life in the thereafter is like. According to those that believe in life after death, there are two places where life after death exists—heaven and hell. Let's try to take a look at the heaven after death life. If there is a life after death in heaven what is it like? Do people sit around and pray all the time and look at their god? Will there be a need to eat, sleep and eliminate? Will you be able to do pleasurable things like having sex or taking a bath? If there is life after death what is the reason for the existence? We articulate that everything has a reason for its actuality.

Upon further reflection, I speculate that there will be no need for bodily functions because your body will remain in the earth. The body in the grave will eventually decompose. It will not accompany you to the afterlife (if there is an afterlife). Minus the body, what is left? The only thing left is the consciousness – your mind. If the consciousness is the only thing left, what is one supposed to do with it? Is the consciousness the thing that religious people call the soul?

There have been as least billions of people that have populated the earth. Are there billions of consciousnesses floating around out there because the earth has been populated with billions of people over the ages? If the consciousness of people who once populated the earth is still out there, what is their purpose and what do they do on a daily basis? We have been taught that everything has a purpose.

Among the many religious theories that exist between the different religions, there is a theory that the body and consciousness will reunite at Judgment Day. Judgment Day is supposed to be the day when life on Earth ends and all people who inhabited the earth will be called (before god) to answer for their behavior in life. But until then, the consciousness of departed people (sometimes called souls) will flout until the god of that religion determines that the world shall end.

Do those conscious exist to influence present day life on earth? There are the good people on earth who were born and raised in a nourishing environment, they loved and were loved. They pass on their genes and make a contribution to the world. They do not violate or harm other people. There are also bad people on earth. Criminals who steal, murder, violate other people, lie, cheat, and are detrimental to society. Is it the job of all those consciousnesses to influence the good and the bad people who are alive today?

I don't know. I'm just asking the questions. For years, I have wondered what the dead do—if there is an afterlife or if they do anything—or if they even exist at all as an entity in an afterlife. My friends who strongly believe in life after death tell me that I have to have faith. I ask them faith in what? They tell me that God's plan takes care of the afterlife and that I should not try to analyze God's plan. They say that I don't need to worry. They tell me if I am a good person, God will take care of me if I have faith in Him. But they can't tell me what there is to do in the thereafter. I really don't expect that they can tell me. Because I don't believe that there is an afterlife and there are no testimonials from the dead.

Artists have drawn pictures of people who they think are in heaven. The pictures drawn depict people in heaven sitting around looking at god. If there is life after death, I hope that there are other things to do besides just sitting around looking at God. People have had an active life. I find it hard to believe that people are just sitting around adoring God all day for eternity. In heaven, do you lose your ability to be active?

The pictures by artists of people in the supposedly hell portray them being thrown into the fires. Is this an all-day activity? The artists are wrong. Remember there are no bodies in the afterlife—the bodies are still on earth, decaying. From time to time we dig up bodies of people who have been dead for ages. Those bodies (skeletons) have been around for a long time. They didn't go anywhere. The flesh rots.

As far as I have seen there are two activities that man has depicted about the afterlife. After dying man has either spent his time sitting around glorifying god or suffering in the fires of Hell? When I die, I hope that whatever it is, it is as challenging as life on earth was challenging— if there is an afterlife.

Throughout the early history of man being on this earth, there has been phenomena that man could not understand or explain. Why did the sky pour down rain? Why did the sun rise and fall? What made the wind blow? Man did not discover atmospheric pressure until many a thousand of years later. These questions and thousand more confronted early man who was naturally inquisitive about his existence and the nature that surrounded him. Man was persistent in his quest for answers. Although he could not explain his surroundings and the marvels of nature that occurred around him, he had to come up with something that would satisfy his quest to explain the marvels of his environment.

Why do men die? For what purpose are men born? Were men reborn after they died? These were among the other questions that had to be asked and solved by man's prying mind. When the inhabitants of earth could not solve the problems that plagued their minds, they came up with a concept that brought solace to their perplexed beings. The comfort that they brought forth was "God." At the time of early man, man could not logically explain his existence or the marvels and wonderment of the natural world around him. So, he invoked the existence of supernatural beings to fill the voids in his mind. Man could not explain the wind and the sun, but he deduced that there was some power that could. Even after he learned to make fire, he theorized that he could not control it when it got out of hand and burned him and his possessions. Man reasoned that there had to be a superior being who could control the things in nature that were beyond the control of man. He also reasoned that he could say some words that would assuage that greater power in an effort to enlist this superior being to solve whatsoever dilemma that was confronting man. Man came up with the concept of prayer or rituals, that sometimes included human sacrifice, to enlist the help of this supernatural being (god) to alleviate man's problems.

Gods existed in the minds of man in prehistory. Prehistory is the period in time before man learned to write and leave a record of things that happened to him. The first recorded written words were in existence about 5000 years ago. In the written records of those times, man wrote about religion and god(s). Religion can be defined as a belief in one or more Gods. Or as man's attempt to align himself with the perceived greatest power in the universe which man named God. Religion is usually a group endeavor. A group of people develop a philosophy for man's existence, and codes of conduct for the followers of that religion to follow.

Early man created a God for everything that he could not control. A God for magic, sun, war, love, agriculture, animals and creation was brought into conception by man's imagination. The creators of God thought that there had to be a specific God for each and everything. If you wanted to win a war you prayed to the god of war. You didn't pray to the God of love to win a war. Worldwide, through various cultures, there were hundreds of Gods created by ancient man. In the countries that constitute South East Asia alone there were over 20 Gods. In ancient Egypt there were 15 gods or more.

When modern men studied ancient cultures, they had no problem admitting that ancient people **created** these Gods to fulfill their need to understand the world as they experienced it in ancient times. Early man **created** a God to cover all circumstances in life and they seriously believed in the Gods that they created. The ancient Greek and Egyptians who were among the world's greatest civilizations at the time of their existence, left copious records of their Gods and the perceived effect that those Gods had on their populous. Every ancient culture had a God or Gods that they worshipped.

Besides the Greeks and Romans there were other ancient cultures that had deities that they believed in. The Incas and the Aztecs in the Americas had their gods as did the occupants on the Indian, African and Asia continents. Many ancient cultures believed that their god lived inside the earth as opposed to being in the havens. The ancient Greeks had at least 15 gods. Some of their gods were:

- Poseidon   God of the Sea
- Hermes   God of Trade
- Ares   God of War
- Zeus   God of the Sky
- Aphrodite   Goddess of Love
- Hera   Goddess of Women
- Artemis   God of the Hunt

The creations of the ancient Gods by ancient man are akin to modern man's creation of superheroes. Gods in ancient days could send thunder bolts through the sky and fly from place to place. Superman and his fellow superheroes of our present-day have those abilities. The only difference between the ancient

Gods and the superheroes is that the superheroes of today are enjoyed as entertainment. They are not worshipped as Gods.

Present day Christians belittle Gods that they call pagan which were believed in by ancient man. Gods of ancient history were dismissed by man after most men accepted the notion that there is only one God. It is claimed by Christians that ancient man was ignorant of the one true God. The people of the ancient era who believed in multiple Gods are no longer with us. They believed in the so called "pagan gods" just as much as modern man believes in the present day one God.

Today, there is a certain religious philosophy, in some cultures, that indicates that you have to acknowledge the one true god in order to receive eternal salvation. Before the present-day god was discovered, most of the people who worshipped pagan gods were dead. There were millions of people who inhabited the earth and venerated those so-called pagan gods. They did not have a chance to acknowledge the "one true God." What was their fate? Are they doomed to what Christians call eternal damnation because they lacked the knowledge of the supposedly true god? Are they the forgotten people? Why didn't the Christians reach back and give those people credit for not being apprised by the god of his existence. If this present-day god is the true god and if god created the early day people, why didn't this god let the people in early history know that he was the true god instead of letting them worship the pagan gods. Why did the one god wait so long to make man knowledgeable of his existence? Those would be serious questions if a god really existed. But because god doesn't really exist, the questions are not relevant.

Some religions, the Catholics in particular, which are Christian, might have come up with an answer to what happened to the people who worshipped the pagan gods before the one true God made himself known to mankind. They have a concept called purgatory. Purgatory is defined by the Catholics as an intermediate place after physical death in which some of those ultimately destined for heaven must first undergo purification. The people who are sent to purgatory must wait in purgatory until the so-called judgment day of the Christians comes about. Can the people who lived before the Christian Church was founded or before the one God concept came into being achieve the holiness necessary to enter their, so called, joy of heaven? If not, what happens to the people who populated the earth and were ignorant, through no fault of their own, of the supposedly one true God before that deity made himself known to man? Are the Catholics/Christians saying that those people will be held in purgatory until judgment day and then their lives will be examined to see if they will be allowed into the kingdom of heaven.

Holding that certain offences that they committed can be forgiven in their time on earth because of their ignorance of God and his laws, can they be given a pass into haven? The above question is a common-sense question that I have not heard religions deal with. Though, I am sure that if the question of the fate of those people came to fore, the religions would find an answer to that dilemma.

There are thousands of questions about religion that can be perplexing to man. At this point, I have only touched on a very few of those queries. Before I dwell on other enquiries about religion, I would like to touch on the concept of religious creativity.

Religious Creativity and Holy Books Written by Man

Recently, I sat with a group of writers who meet regularly. We were discussing other writers' work. During the discussion we were praising and admiring the work of those writers who produce script for television shows. We acknowledged that the writers for the television series are indeed talented. They are required to come up with new material each week and they do it. Rarely, if ever, do they duplicate material from past programs of theirs or other writers unless they were making a remake of a past program. Even so, if they made a rewrite, they usually put in new material or come up with a new twist into the remake. We gave those writers their accolades and adjourned our meeting.

As I left the meeting, I begun to think of other writers besides those that write for the current television programs. My mind took me back to the time when I was born in the thirties, when radio was the principle media for everyday America. Programs such as *The Shadow*, *The Lone Ranger*, *Abbott and Costello*, *Gang Busters*, *Sam Spade -Detective*, *The Aldridge*

Family, to name a few, were radio programs that captivated American audiences at the time. Radio and the movies employed numerous writers to come up with scripts for those entertainment pieces. The writing tradition continues today for the entertainment industry. Every media program comes up with new material, molded by the new writers. The material created by writers follows a tradition of writers from the past throughout the ages. From the time that man learned to write, man has used his skill to write stories and to recall and mix history with their interpretation. Fiction coupled with history is standard fare for writers. The ability to use their imagination and creativity is an integral skill employed by writers.

Although, the writer's tradition didn't start with the writers that wrote the Bible, those authors of the Bible wrote enduring pieces that have lasted throughout the ages. The Bible is one of the oldest, most often mentioned creative pieces of enduring written art that man has created. The Bible is full of man's work at his best with the use of fact and fiction. The combination of using fact and fiction is a skill that writers have applied to their works over the ages before the Bible was written.

One of the most often mentioned Biblical works is the story of Noah's Ark. According to the story contained in Genesis, God told Noah that He was troubled because man was wicked and He (God) regretted making human beings. He told Noah that He would wipe from the face of the earth, the human race that he had created. He must have changed his mind because the Bible then said that God told Noah that Noah was a righteous man and He would spare Noah and his family. By saying this, god intended to spare Noah so that he and his family could start a new blood line of earthlings after God had destroyed the other inhabitants of the earth including the animals, the plants and fish in the sea. The passage does not indicate what problems God had with the animals, the plants and the fish but it was his intention to destroy them all—so says the works in the Bible about what God said. It was a good story line to this point and now the reader's interest is captured to see how God is going to bring about this destruction. Is it going to be by fire, water, an explosion or is God going to suck the air from the earth? The writers of the piece had God choose water as His instrument of mass destruction.

The story continued with God notifying Noah of the watery destruction method to come and informing Noah that he needed to build a boat (The Ark) so that he and his family could survive the impending flood that would wipe out all living things on the earth including the fish in the water. This is one of the first uses of hyperbole in the story—when the authors indicate that the fishes in the sea will be destroyed by water, but that's what is contained in the book in which Christians call The Holy Bible.

The Bible says that God tells Noah to gather every animal species on earth and put them into his boat. The location of the story appears to be somewhere in the Middle East. Eventually, after the flood waters recede the Ark lands on Mount Ararat which is in present-day Turkey. I skipped to the ending of the story because I have often wondered where in the Middle East, did Noah find a polar bear or a gorilla and how did he get a whale into the Ark. Many parts of the world had not been discovered when the Ark was supposed to have existed. I guess that those animals in the world unknown to man survived the flood without Noah's assistance. There are versions of the story that indicate that God brought the animals to Noah.

In some versions of the story it states that it took Noah 120 years to build the Ark. The authors of the account of Noah and the Ark put Noah's age at 480 years when he started to build the Ark and at 600 years old when the Ark was completed. Noah was said to have three sons and a wife. Their ages are not given in the account. The authors of the story do not give the ages of Noah's family, but they leave it to the reader's imagination to speculate on the family's ages. Wow, people lived to be 600 years old in those days and only have three children! Noah's age, the amount of time that it took to build the Ark and the gathering of the animals puts the story in the fictional category.

The part about the flood is conceivable. There are floods throughout the history of the world. So, an author took license with the fact that the world experiences floods and added a fictional piece to build a story that has caught the fancy of many people in the world and was included in a work that is full of fantasy: The Bible.

In my critique of the Biblical piece of Noah, I would be remiss if I did not touch on another Biblical entry that writers put energy into, and it became part of the best seller of all time–the Bible.

The story of Adam and Eve was taught as a fact when I was raised in the Catholic faith as a youngster. Everybody knows the story of how God created man, Adam, and then created woman from the rib of Adam. Anthropology has since taught us that it couldn't have happened that way. But let's give the believers in the story, the benefit of the doubt and say that it happened that way. The Bible tells us that the first man and woman were thrown out of paradise because they ate a forbidden fruit and one of the persons lied about it to God. In the story, Adam and Eve incurred the wrath of God for stealing and lying and God expelled them from the Garden for these infractions.

But this God is portrayed by other writers as supposedly a forgiving God. Why couldn't this God, who is espoused as the loving patriarch, overlook this transgression? It's conceivable to think that god could have been benevolent in that instance. If God would have forgiven the perpetrators of this act, he would have spared the world from much suffering.

When the story was written, the world had existed for millions of years and the writers had seen or knew of the hardships that man had experienced since creation. The writers could not make God into a compassionate being in the Garden of Eden drama. They needed to give a reason for man's pitiful plight since the affair in the Garden. According to the writers of the Bible every bad thing that has happened to man can be traced to Adam and Eve. But no one has written the story about why God's animosity lasted so long and why did He had His creations suffer so much before He appeared to mankind and put them on the path to what is called salvation? Well, again, it's just a well written story that the original writers had success in selling to a public that wanted to believe in a concrete tale about the creation of man and man's lost favor with God.

The question that the writers did not address was why did this God who created Adam and Eve and thus mankind, let them leave the Garden of Eden without keeping in touch with them? When man left the Garden in his dumbness, he created those pagan Gods and worshipped those pagan Gods for centuries before this supposedly true God came along and made himself known to man—again. I would have thought that this God would have kept in touch with his creations so that he could have kept mankind out of the troubles that man eventually experienced. But remember it's an entertainment piece created by talented writers.

One more biblical tale that has seen much popularity over the centuries since it was written is the Exodus. This is the story of Moses who led his people, the Israelites, out of bondage in Egypt. The Israelites had been the slaves of the Egyptians for a long period of time and as the story goes the Israelites were Gods chosen people. Why weren't all men God's chosen people since God is purported to have created Man? That's another question that has not been answered to my satisfaction.

Anyway, the story has Moses leading his people out of Egypt with the Egyptian army in hot pursuit. Moses comes to the Red Sea and his route of escape is blocked because he needs to get across the Red Sea to the Promised Land. There are at least four different versions of how he accomplishes that feat. The most popular version has Moses putting out his staff and God lets him part the sea and make a path for the escape of the Israelites. That's the movie version.

Upon research, I found out that there are three more versions, written by different authors, of Moses' escape. One version has God clogging the wheels of the Egyptian army's chariots so that they cannot pursue the fleeing multitudes of liberated slaves. Another version has God, without Moses sticking out his staff, blowing a strong East wind allowing the Israelites to cross on dry land. The third version has God casting the Egyptians into a mystical abyss, which the Bible describes as a place of waste and void. In two of the versions the Egyptians do not even enter the water.

The above entries from the Bible are samples of the many stories contained in that body of work where writers, sometimes called prophets, have taken freedom to construct stories that have survived throughout the ages because man thirsts for accounts of his beginnings and man also thirsts for understanding of those unknown origins. And it doesn't hurt that it is entertaining!

The vast majority of Christianity has accepted the writings in The Bible, the Quran and books of other religions as fact because it helps them coup with things that they do not understand in life. It appears that it is hard for man to accept the notion that they don't know why things happen in the world, so they are willing to accept stories like the creation of the world in 7 days as outlined in their Bible.

But these and other stories in The Bible, the Quran and other religious books are indoctrinated in the minds of young and old as if they were facts. As a youngster, I was brainwashed to believe the stories were indeed fact and the indoctrinators put the scare in me to believe that if I did not accept them as truth, I would be sentenced to eternal damnation.

The Inquisition

As time has progressed, human beings have come to discover why thing in the natural world work the way they do because of discoveries in science. Hundreds of years ago Galileo, the Italian scientist, was convicted of heresy by the Catholic Church. The church put together special courts to examine what they called heretics. A Heretic is defined as a dissenter from established church dogma. Every religion has some form of dogma which they postulate to their membership. If the membership expresses disbelief in the religious dogma, those members are branded as heretics or the heretic equivalent for whatever religion is in question. Modern religions are not the only religions that condemned its people who doubted the religious teaching of its religious leaders. The ancients also put people to death who went against the established beliefs.

In the 1500s, the Catholic Church was predominant in Europe. Galileo who was a scientist researching astrometry was sentenced to house arrest because he said the planets revolved around the sun. In that day in age, The Catholic dogma had the earth as the center of the universe. All heavenly bodies were supposed to revolve around the earth. The catholic dogma indicated that the earth was the center of the universe and the other celestial bodies revolved around the earth.

The Church did not accept other definitions of the operation of the world. Galileo and other scientists proved the church wrong, but it took the stubborn church a long period of time to accept scientific fact about the makeup of the universe. If one went against the teaching of the church, you were deemed a heretic and many a heretic was burned at the stake for going against the church's beliefs.

There was a period in time called The Inquisition when many persons were executed by burning at the stake for disagreeing with the church's philosophy. The Inquisition took place in Europe. After the Christian church became established in most parts of Europe, the teachings of the church were regarded as the foundation of law and order. The government and the church were one. There was no separation between Church and State. What the church said and what the government said was the accepted law of the land. Kings ruled the country and all of the kings were Catholic and they relied on their Bishops for input from Rome. Rome was the center of the religion and the Pope who was the leader of the Catholic faith was considered to be infallible when it came to delivering church dogma.

If one went against the philosophy of the church, you were considered a heretic, which was akin to being a criminal. You could be excommunicated from the church for going against church doctrine, which in the language of Christianity meant that you were destined for hell.

In the centuries since The Inquisition, the Christian religion has accepted many facts of science that men were put to death for in the early history of the church. Joan of Arc, a French hero in the fight against the English, was deemed a heretic and was burned at the stake for her beliefs and actions. The church later admitted that an error was made in branding her a heretic and made her a saint. Has the church ever admitted that the story of God creating the universe and man in seven days is a myth? In my catechism class in grade school, the Creation story was taught as a rock-solid truth. I'll later compare the church version of creation of the earth with the scientific version of creation.

The Muslim faith also had its version of The Inquisition and today Muslim dogma has not changed to the extent that it accepts the changes necessary to make life on earth for people who believe in their Faith more satisfying. Women do not have the same status as men in Muhammad's faith. But who am I to say that Muslim women are not satisfied with their status? Although recently, the world was shown the joy that those women experienced when the Muslim Country of Saudi Araba lifted the religious ban on driving and let women drive to work.

I have mentioned the word faith a number of times since I began writing this book. Faith is the bedrock that religion is based upon. Faith is the important element of religion because much of religious dogma cannot be proven such as the existence of God. There are a few definitions offered in the Bible and in other sources of the meaning of faith. Let's take a look at some meanings that are given to the word.

Faith

One definition of faith in the Christian Bible defines faith as "the ***substance*** of things hoped for, evidence of things not seen."[1] Faith is the belief in things that we hope for but have not yet received. Faith (confidence, belief, trust) is also our evidence of that which is not seen—the invisible thing. Faith comes before a prayer to God is answered or before an individual has received what he or she has requested from God. If we receive what we wish for, then faith is not needed. So says the Bible.

I tried to translate the above from the Bible into something that I, as a lay person can understand. The way that I interpret the above definition of faith is:

> Let us say that I hope for a new car. According to the above, I trigger faith by making a **prayer to a God** in an effort to get the car (**The substance**). I put all my trust, belief and confidence in God that he will answer my prayer so that I can get the car (using the Bible's definition). I get the car and once I have the car, I no longer need faith because my prayers were answered. Faith was the invisible **substance** that cannot be seen but it got me the car.

---

[1] Hebrews 11:1 KJV

That would be one take on trying to use faith in my life as proposed by the Bible.

My above translation of faith leaves me a bit confused. Here is the way that I have used faith in my life time. I have wanted a new car during my existence. I did not pray to God to get the new car. I did have **faith** in that I would be able to get the car. The **substance** of my faith came from knowing that I would be able to purchase the vehicle if I had a job that paid a salary which would allow me to have funds to afford payments. The **substance** of my hope and faith was a job and funds to procure the thing. There were also so-called **substances,** as outlined in the Bible, that I had before I even knew that I wanted to purchase that particular car. They were having an intellect and an education or experience that would allow me to procure employment that allowed me to purchase the car and it all occurred without praying to a God

I hope that the above made sense to the reader. As a lay person, I am trying to define faith whereby it makes more sense than just praying to an invisible God. I think that faith can have visible **substance**. I understand that there are those that have faith in a God as their main source of living. I have faith in my limited ability to affect my life. Things happen in life whether or not you have faith. I fell and almost broke my hand. People get run over by cars and get hit by stray bullets every day. There was no faith involved in those happening. One could pray and have faith that those things don't happen to them. I say you are lucky if you go through life unscathed. In having that belief, I come into contradiction with some of the Catholic Church's greatest thinkers.

There have been many attempts to demonstrate the existence of God by philosophical arguments. Many men have attained the title of philosopher. There was a philosopher by the name of Anselm. He was originally from Italy. He was a Catholic priest in France. He lived in the 11th Century. A priest is a professional clergyman of a religious domination. Anselm was promoted from a priest to a Bishop and sent to England. A Bishop is a member of the Christian cleric hierarchy who is in charge of a vast segment of the Church's population. Bishops are empowered with positions of authority. When the king of England in the 11th Century refused to recognize the freedom of the church from the king's control, Anselm opposed the king and he had to go into exile. Exile means he was run out of England. Later, when a new king came to the throne in England, Anselm was able to return to England and resume his Bishop duties because the new King submitted to the authority of the Church.

Anselm was a Religious philosopher. He was credited by the Catholic Church with giving the accepted explanation for the existence of God through Faith. After his death he was made a Saint for his supportive religious philosophies and his defense of the Catholic Church.

After reading the Anselm explanation of the existence of Faith and God, it took the better part of two weeks to try and understand his accepted proof of the existence of God. I needed to understand what Anselm was saying in order to agree or not agree with his conclusions about faith and the existence of God. Philosophers used exalted language and one needs to be sure of what the philosopher has written and is trying to convey. Anselm's theology is very confusing but after a time of study, I came to the conclusion that his treatise on faith came down to this. I am going to quote the meat of it. He says

> "God cannot be thought of as nonexistence because you can think of God - and if you can think of God you cannot think of anything greater then God. If you can think of something that exists then it has to exist once you have thought of a thing existing. You cannot think that God cannot exist because you (have already) thought of his existence - so God cannot be thought of as nonexistent." [2]

Anselm also argues "That because you can think of God you cannot think of anything greater than God."[3] I understand that Anselm is saying that faith can be a belief in the existence of a thing with or without proof that the thing exists.

Based upon the above and his defense of the Catholic Church, Anselm was rewarded after his death. He received the highest honor that can be bestowed upon a member of the Church. He became a Saint. We will talk about sainthood later. The Church relied on Anselm's definition of the proof of God for

---

[2] Thomas A. Shipka and Arthur J. Minton, *Philosophy Paradox and Discovery,* (McGraw-Hill, 1997) p24
[3] Ibid.

centuries even in the face of other learned men's rejection of his tract.

I don't consider myself as a learned man, but I think that I can contradict Anselm's discourse on faith and God. He said that if you think of something then it must exist because you have thought of it. Ok, I can think of a building or a horse or me flying by its own power, or of me throwing a baseball 200 miles per hour. But because I can think of that kind of a phenomena, it doesn't make it true. I have an imagination which allows me to think of all kind of things but because I can think of a thing, it doesn't make it a reality. None of those objects can fly on their own just because I can think it.

Of all of the church's philosophers, I picked Anselm's works to critique because I have a connection with the Saint. I went to St Anselm's elementary school located on the south side of Chicago. I went as far as the 8th grade before I got kicked out for running away from home.

I had a cruel foster mother who was going to administer another beating and I ran. The priest did not sympathize with a 12-year-old who was terrorized in foster care, so I had to finish elementary school in the public schools. I did get into a Catholic high school but was again kicked out because I would not allow the priest to administer corporal punishment to me.

I eventually finished secondary education in another Catholic High School at Father Flanagan's - Boys Town High School in Boys Town, Nebraska. I went to church every morning of my high school days. After graduation from high school, I have only entered a church for a wedding or a funeral out of respect for the participants. At eighteen years old, I was through with religious philosophy.

Religions and Religious Faiths[4]

There are numerous religions and religious faiths around the world. Wikipedia indicates that there are over 4,000 different religions in the world. I understand that most people need to believe in God because there is a lot in life that is not understandable, and they need to believe that there is something after their life on earth is over. Because of those needs, they are willing to accept the existence of a superior being who they have faith in and to join groups that postulate and promote the superior being that looks out for them. Then, there are those that do not believe in a god or in a life after death. What separates the two? It has to be faith or a lack of faith in a god. Some people are attached to religions that have various beliefs. There are a range of beliefs and faith in those beliefs across different religions. Participants practice their faith using various methods.

Let us take a look at some of the religions around the world and see what they stand for, what they believe in, what they all have in common and also what are some of the differences.

Christianity, a world religion, believes that a single creator, God, had a son, Jesus Christ, born of a human mother,

---

[4] Wikipedia; "Major Religious Groups."

and that Jesus's crucifixion and resurrection brings about salvation and that Jesus is God. There are many denominations associated with Christianity. Within the Christian religion, there are a range of different beliefs. Some of the different denominations are Baptist, Lutheran, Methodist, Catholic, Calvinist, and The Episcopal Church etc. Christianity is associated with the conquering, theft of land, the conversion of the natives to Christianity and enslavement of people on the African, Americas and the Australian Continents.

Islam believes that Allah is god, Mohammad was the prophet and Jesus Christ was a messenger in the religion of Allah. The Holy Book of Islam, The Quran, denies that Jesus was crucified and denies that he arose from the dead and also denies that Jesus is a God in the Islam Religion.

Heaven's Gate is an apocalyptic suicide religious cult that combined the Biblical purpose of the world with new age ideas about UFOs. Its entire congregation—39 members—committed suicide in 1997.

Confucianism is an ethics-based world religion whose disciples practice and cultivate cardinal virtues of piety, kindness, righteousness, propriety, intelligence, and faithfulness. The religion is based on a collection of ethical and moral teachings. A God is not foremost in this religion.

Brahman Kaman is a religion preparing to rule the world after the coming apocalypse.

Buddhism is a world religion. This religion believes that man is being continually reincarnating after death. A belief that meditation and good living can break the cycle of reincarnation and result in a enlighten man. The world will end when the cycle of reincarnation ends.

Hinduism is a world religion of India which was historically decentralized and dissimilar and not a single belief system. Western influence (especially from England) made it revert into a single religion which Hindus now accept. Reincarnation is a part of the Hindu religion. One dies and is rebirthed.

Gnosticism is religion that believes we must escape this world which was created and is ruled by an inferior and unworthy god and reunite with the true god (Whoever that is). People needed secret knowledge to be freed from the material world which is inherently evil.

Brahman Kumara is religion also preparing to rule the world after the apocalypse.

Shinto is a religion in Japan. The emperor used to be its living God until Japan was defeated in World War II.

Voodoo is a traditional religion from Haiti with an ethical focus on combating greed and promoting humor. Voodoo is ostracized by various other religions.

Zhu Shen Jiao, a Chinese folk religion, established a kingdom of God. In the approach to 2000 its leaders were arrested amid fears that it would turn into a suicide cult.

The Peoples Temple is a paranoid church led by a Methodist minister, Jim Jones, who fought for civil rights for Black people and led its congregation to Central America. Jones held the membership captive, killed a US Congressman and then got his followers to committee suicide by drinking Kool Aid.

Hookers for Jesus is a sexually promiscuous group who fell under police suspicion. Increasing pressure from outside resulted in the group retreating further into insanity and they became The Family, predicting the end of the world.

Scientology, derived from the writings of L Ron Hubbard, is a series of practices called Dianetics which is used to clear minds of alien influences and attain a state of mental perfection.

Jehovah's Witnesses believe God will clean the earth of wickedness in the near future and reintroduce the paradise conditions that He intended for the human race in the beginning. Only a little flock of 144,000 will go to heaven and rule with Christ. There is an impending apocalypse, and man's time is near the end.

As seen from the sampling above, there are many religions and many religious faiths and beliefs in the world. Members of each faith, belief, cult, church, synagogue or place of worship believe in the trueness of their god. Most religions today believe in the one god concept but there are still some religions that have a multiply god concept. Christianity believes in one God and that God had a son named Jesus and the religion allows you to worship the son of God. There is another character in the religion named the Holy Spirit, whose name was changed from the Holy Ghost.

When I was young, Catholics used to pray to God the Father, God the Son and God the Holy Ghost. I believe that there was a name change from the Holy Ghost to the Holy Spirit because it was not too modern sounding to pray to a ghost (that's my take).

The Catholics are also allowed to pray to the Saints in their religion. I believe that Saint praying is allowed because Catholics believe the Saints can be intermediaries between man and God. Saints are a special category established in the Catholic Church.

In order to attain sainthood, one has to be dead and be designated for sainthood by the church. The designee must have been accredited with causing two to three miracles. An example of a miracle in the consideration of the Catholic Faith for Sainthood is when a person who is deafly sick, beyond medical help, prays to a Saint candidate for a cure. If the person recovers, the Catholic Church declares that the reason for the recovery was the prayer made to the person who is a candidate to become a saint. Thus, when the prayer is answered, as evident by the recovery, the recovery is credited as a miracle performed by the dead Saint Candidate. The Church then declares that the prayer to the Saint Candidate and the resulting cure was one of the needed miracles to be counted for the candidate to become a Saint. Some of the church's faithful revolted against the church's practice of canonizing saints because they viewed worshipping saints as worshipping other images besides god.

Christianity's Revolt

The Lutherans, Baptist, Methodist, and Calvinist are Christians but are considered Protestants. The word protestant is derived from the word 'protest' which means that the religions that are deemed protestant protested the Catholic faith and broke away because they disagreed with the philosophy of the Catholic Church.

Martin Luther, who founded the Lutheran Church in1517, indicated that he thought that the Catholic Papacy, which is located in Rome and is where the leadership of the Catholic Church resides, was corrupt because it was selling indulgences to the rich within the religion. The practice of indulgences meant that the wealthy could pay a sum to the church and they would be forgiven of their sins and could attain forgiveness and the Catholic Church kingdom of heaven. Luther rebelled against the practice and formed his own church. In the ensuing years, a wave of priests followed Martin Luther's example and protested against the practices of the Catholic Church. The rebel priests thought that the Catholics Hierarchy in Rome was more interested in making money then in saving souls. The breakaway priests established their own brands of Christianity.

It is evident that the vast majority of people on the Earth need to believe and have faith in some power greater than themselves. Most people belong to and seek guidance from some type of religious organization. Believers cannot categorize themselves as not understanding. As noted above, there are over 4,000 such religious organizations worldwide. Most world cultures, whether large or small, have religious organizations associated with the culture. A culture is defined as the total pattern of human behavior and its products - in thought, speech, action, knowledge and artifacts which are handed down to succeeding generations through the use of tools, language and system of abstract thought.[5] In most instances from the time one is born until the time of death; humans are indoctrinated with some form of religious philosophy. Although religious Philosophy differs from one religion to another, there are some aspects in religion that are common to all faiths.

Common Religious Beliefs Are:

- Religions believe that there is a superior or supreme being who is all powerful
- Most, if not all religions, believe that there is some form of a life after death
- Religions have ethical beliefs and religious rituals that are the most public manifestation of the religion such as services, parades, feasts etc.

---

[5] Wikipedia, "List of Religions and Spiritual Traditions."

- Reverence, morality, loyalty are included in religious thesis as religions outline what they stand for.
- Religions have a sense of community that provides for the group cohesion and identity. They gather their flock in churches, mosques, temples, synagogues etc.[6]

Other Religions Similarities

Two religions that have fought and killed many members of each sect are the Christians and Muslims. It would be more appropriate to say that the Catholic and Muslim sects had warred against each other for Centuries. The crusades in the 11th and 12th Centuries, sponsored by the Catholic Countries of Europe, were an attempt to recapture the so-called Holy Lands from the Muslims. The Holy Lands that were the targets of the Christian crusades are in the Middle Eastern part of the world. The City of Jerusalem was the target of the crusaders. The Christians indicated that the Holy Lands were where Christianity started, and that the Muslim faith should not be in control of the sacred places of the Christian religion. Today the Muslims and the Jews are in dispute over those same places.

The two religions have a lot in common. Christianity and Islam have many similarities, but the similarities have major differences. As stated earlier, Jesus Christ is in both religions. Both religions are defined by the presence of Jesus Christ. The Christians believe that Jesus Christ is a God. The Muslims think that Christ is a messenger of the Muslim God, Allah. In the

---

[6] Wikipedia, "Comparative Religion."

Christian's Bible, in Romans 10.9 it states, "If you declare with your mouth 'Jesus is Lord' and believe in your heart that God raised him from the dead you will be saved."

Therefore, in order to be saved in Christianity, there are three components one must agree with in order to be saved. You must

(1) believe that Jesus Christ died by crucifixion,

(2) believe that Jesus Christ arose from the dead, and

(3) believe that Jesus Christ is God.

In the Muslim faith they believe that Jesus Christ existed, however, they

(1) deny Christ died by crucifixion

(2) deny Christ was resurrected after death, and

(3) believe Jesus never claimed that He was God.

The Quran, which is the Muslim Holy Book and is the foundation of the Muslim faith, denies Jesus' death by crucifixion. The Muslims believe that the Quran is the expression of God and in 4.157[7], the Quran states Jesus was a Messenger of Allah (The Muslim God). Allah did not let them kill Jesus, nor

---

[7] And their saying "We killed the Messiah, Jesus son of Mary, the Messenger of God " – whereas they did not kill him, nor did they crucify him, but the matter was made dubious to them. Those who differ about this matter and about Jesus are indeed confused; they have no definite knowledge thereof, following mere conjecture; and of a certainty, they killed him not.

did they crucify him, but they made (it) to appear so. The Muslim faith indicated that Allah substituted a person to die on the cross for Christ. In the Muslim faith they believe that Allah did not let Christ die on Earth, but that Allah raised Christ, the Messenger, to heaven—still alive.

Jesus Christ is many times mentioned in The Muslim Holy Book, The Quran. He is mentioned as a Prophet, as are Abraham, Noah and Moses—names from the Old Testament Bible.

The Quran is the basis of the Muslim faith. Millions of people believe in the Muslin version. Also, millions of people believe in the Christian version. The Buddhist, The Hindus and other major religion groups are not concerned with Jesus Christ because they have their own Gods.

Religious Backing of Enslavement

Throughout the history of the world, most religions have condoned slavery at some time. Today, it is thought that slavery would be against the ethics of most religions. That was not so in earlier times of religious involvement.

It is thought that one of the ways that slavery started in the world was through warfare. A group of people would war with another group of people and the winning group would enslave the defeated group. Since some form of religion has always been associated with groups or cultures of people, the religious people of the group had been tasked to come up with morals for the group to live by. The religious leaders had excused and tolerated slavery on one premise or another. There is a passage in the Bible that says "Obey your master" which infers that there has always been a master slave relationship in the world of the Christian religion.

The way the world works it can be easily seen why the religious person in the culture did not rule that slavery should be against the morals of the group. The religious person in the group was normally associated with the group leadership and benefitted from free labor of the slaves. Slavery has always been about economics. Economics is about profits and someone profits from slave labor.

The American experience with slavery was tightly entwined with religion. During Slavery, southerners wrapped themselves around the Bible and claimed that because they thought that the Bible indicated that Black people were an inferior race, God sanctioned Blacks as being slaves. In the North of the country, most religious practioners were against slavery. A war had to be fought and over 600,000 American men died before the country could eliminate the practice. Slavery has been present in all cultures and it has been only in recent history that many religions have come out against the evil practice.

Catholicism was the dominant religion on the European continent up to and into the 16th Century. Spain was firmly put into the Catholic mold in 1492 when the Spanish rulers expelled Muslim rulers from the part of Spain that had been under the control of Islam. Islam had conquered and occupied the Spanish Peninsula in the 8th Century.

In 1517, the protestant reformation hit Europe. It was started by Martin Luther, a Catholic priest. A number of other so-called reformers left the Catholic Church and established Christian Denomination churches of their own. For one reason or another, they began to disagree with the philosophy of the Pope and the Catholic Church. The reformers opposed such doctrine as the merits of the Saints or the forgiveness of sins by indulgence. Indulgence was the paying for forgiveness of sins by the rich. The poor had not the means to pay to have their sins forgiven. If one died with sins not forgiven, they were destined for Hell. So said the Catholic Church.

The development of the protestant churches had its effect on the Catholic Church because as the years went by, numbers of the faithful left Roman Catholicism for protestant sects. The church desired to refill the ranks because of the loss of members to the protestant religions. Portugal and Spain were staunchly Catholic countries. They were the leaders in undertaking voyages of discovery to the African and American continents. Besides the material riches on the lands that were uncovered by the explorations, the explores encountered the native people. From the beginning of the engagement with the indigenous people, the explorers used the native people as slaves to rape the land of precious wealth and for their own comforts.

Spain and Portugal were the leading exploring countries in the world in the 14th and 15th centuries. Portuguese sailors explored to the south of the Atlantic Ocean and on the coast of West Africa. Spanish sailors went west from Europe on the

Atlanta Ocean on their voyages of discovery. After discovering the Caribbean islands and the Americas, their armies conquered most of Central and South America. The Spaniards looted the gold and silver of Mexico and Peru, established plantations to grow sugar in the Caribbean and enslaved the native populations to work those plantations.

Spain, being a Catholic country, converted the native population of the conquered lands to Catholicism after they enslaved the population. The Spaniards were adding souls for the church regardless that the souls were slaves. Missionaries were anxious to come to the new world to get into the business of converting the natives. They had the natives build monasteries and churches and used the natives as slaves, servants and sexual objects for the comfort of the priests. Catholic priests, who are supposed to be celibate, used their power to commit fornication with the native population.

The Portuguese also explored the new land discoveries in South America. They laid claim to lands, south of the land claimed by the Spaniards and they wanted to challenge the Spaniards for the lands that the Spaniards had already laid claim to. The main land that the Portuguese laid claim to is present day Brazil. The Spaniards and the Portuguese were involved in disputes over the land claims. In an effort to prevent war—since both were Catholic countries—they submitted their claims to the Vatican. The Catholic Church is headquartered at the Vatican in Rome, Italy. They let the Pope, who is head of the church, mediate the dispute. The Pope drew a line of demarcation on the map and awarded everything north of the line to Spain and land south of the line went to Portugal. When the Pope drew the line settling the dispute, he knew that slavery was being practiced in the disputed lands. The Pope issued a proclamation which deemed that the native population should not be enslaved, yet he was ignored and the practice of slavery continued in the conquered countries with the approval of the Church's hierarchy in America to further the economic interest of the countries involved plus the economic interest of the Catholic Church. The Churches coffers reaped the benefits of stolen wealth and enslaved people in the early years of colonization in the Americas. The Church Bishops in the Americas who ignored the Pope said that they did everything with the approval of God and in the name of Jesus, so according to the Christian Church their God approved slavery.

The Catholic country of Portugal also was a leader in the slave trade involving Africa. There explorers went up and down the coast of West Africa building forts to hold captured Black Africans for export to the Americas. Before the English, the Dutch, the French and other Christian European countries became involved in the slave trade, the Portuguese had led the way in raping and stealing Africa's human resources. At one time or another every known religion has sanctioned slavery.

Besides stealing the natural resources and enslaving the population of Mexico, the Caribbean, Central America and South America, the Spanish also brought diseases to those populations that the natives had no immunities for. Large numbers of the populations of Central and South America and the Caribbean were wiped out as a result of the inability of their people to cope with the diseases brought to their lands by the Europeans. The Europeans needed to replace the native slave laborers that were succumbing to the diseases. Black Africans were found to be able to withstand the viruses and infections that killed the native populations in the Americas and in the Caribbean, so millions of slaves were kidnapped to the Americas to replace the dwindling native populations. The Black Africans could be worked to death and replacements could be obtained from the endless supply of Black Africans in Africa. The Spanish and the Portuguese sent Catholic missionaries to convert the natives and the slaves to Christianity.

When the Protestant countries of Europe—the Netherlands, England, Belgium and Germany—became involved in the colonization movement, they also became slavers and their religious beliefs supported the enslavement of indigenous people.

Religion, God, and the Devil

Man has a need for groups that espouse for the improvement, safety and the passing of culture from generation to generation. People have always come together, around the world, at all times during man's existence on earth, to form organizations to develop ethics, modes of behavior and safety plans for their betterment. Most groups come into existence to develop actions to ensure the survival of the group and its future. Over the ages, groups have developed plans to feed their people, to protect the group from natural disasters such as wind, rain and fire, and protect themselves from outward aggressions. These groups are formed with the idea in mind to do unequivocal good for their participants.

Man has always understood that there are issues on this earth that man does not understand and cannot control. Because he did not understand those issues and because he had a need for some explanation, he invented a supernatural being that he could ask for help, to give him answers to the things he could not comprehend. Thus, **man created god or gods**, so when man could not understand a thing, man could attribute the responsibility to his creation: god.

Remember all of the gods man created in ancient times? Modern man rejected all of those gods that his predecessors had created and came up with the "one true God" concept about 2000 years ago. Man reasoned that a God could explain some of the unanswerable things man encounters while living in a perplexing world. Man wanted to know

- why he was born
- why he had to die
- why some men had more good fortune than others
- how to best use the earth's natural resources
- what life after death is like
- did everyone qualify to be reborn again
- what did it take to qualify for a life in the hereafter
- where did one reside after death

These questions and others were tackled by groups of men who came together and formatted a structure to deal with the unanswered questions that surfaced as a result of man living in a confusing world. The name of that structure is religion. As stated before, Religion is defined as a cultural system of designated behaviors, practices, prophecies, ethics or organizations that relate humanity to the supernatural, transcendental or spiritual element.[8]

The key factor in religion is that it involves the supernatural. Man went as far as he could go with trying to figure out his existence and the answers to the problems that he encountered. When man had exhausted his ability to solve questions, **man invented god or gods**. Man could now use his imagination to give to God powers that were impossible for man to have or comprehend.

Man designated God as creator of the universe. Everything good that happened to man was attributed to God. Man did not want to tarnish the reputation of this good God that he had created, so man also created his counterpart—the Devil. Man could not let his good God be responsible for man's bad behavior. So, the Devil became responsible for the wickedness within man. Man had always encountered wicked, debauched and cruel things in the world. Now, everything that man did that was wrong or evil was attributed to the influence of the sinful Devil.

When man created this supernatural being–God–he also created codes of ethics which he gave God credit for bringing into

---

[8] Wikipedia, "Religion."

existence. Ethics, such as the 10 Commandments in the Christian religion, were allegedly given to man by God.

The creation of ethics in religion is a good and useful thing and has helped the world advance and be a better place for human existence. But couldn't man have developed ethics and morals without the assistance of God(s)? Yes, he could, and he did. It seems that man, apparently unbeknownst to him, did all of the things that he gave credit and attributed to God.

If religion could be stripped of God and the supernatural, there would still be a need for such an organization to exist to solve the world's problems. Man could still come together and do what they do to solve their problems, as they have done since they have been on earth. They would continue to rack their brains for improvements to their survival on earth without the assistance of a mystical being.

There are still a host of problems that need to be solved but the involvement of God in the problem-solving process only slows down finding the solutions to those problems.

Take the earth's population problem as an example. Population control is a problem that exists in many parts of the world. Man has the ability to limit the number of people to be in line with the given resources available to support a given population. Through the use of birth control pills and other devises invented by man, man can prevent contraception. Abortion can terminate pregnancies that have already started. The use of the above methods can and are used to control the world's populations.

China determined that its population was going to out strip the country's ability to feed its people. The government made the decision to limit its population by allowing its couples to have only one child. China did not have to worry about offending a religious sect when it made the decision. China is not a god-fearing country. As a communist country, it is not involved with a God concept that influences its behavior. Its moral and ethical concept was to look out for the welfare of its citizens and according to the Chinese Government it fulfilled its obligation by the 'One Child' edict. The decision was based upon the availably of present and future resources of the country.

Many religions support some form of birth control. The Catholic Church is a major exception. The Catholic Church dictates that man cannot interfere with the natural progression of conception and that the use of any contraption to prevent or abort pregnancy is a sin against their God. The only allowable birth control method that is acceptable to the Catholic faith is the rhythm method, whereby intercourse is abstained from during the period when one could become pregnant.

In the parts of the world where birth control is known and is available, it is widely used. Catholic dogma against birth control methods is one area where the Church fights a losing battle with its flock. Its parishioners no longer want to have 9 and 10 children like in the olden days. Catholics use methods of birth control because people have determined that they can have a better life for themselves and their children if they limit the number of offspring they have. Their use of birth control has nothing to do with the overpopulation of the area that they live in. They use birth control to limit the children that they have to better the enjoyment that they receive in life. This is one instant when the church cannot use faith to stop common sense.

Religion, Ethics and Extermination

Religion with its belief in the supernatural has been present and will remain a force in man's life. Most men believe in God and those men believe that everything that happens in life is influenced by God or his nemesis, the Devil. Man prays to God, wishes to God, and hopes to God through his religion and the beliefs established by the religion. Religious groups are involved in the establishment of norms and ethics for societies and nations. There is a need for assemblies within society to push for improvements, safety and the passing of culture from generation to generation. People come together around the world and form organizations to develop ethics and modes of behavior for the betterment of their societies. There are civic and government groups that involve themselves in this principle work. Most groups, not all, that come into existence are influenced by a religious philosophy. The aim of these groups is to do what they believe is unequivocal good work for their societies by developing ethics and behavior that will advance their culture.

Virtuous ethics in the minds of some groups is cruel for other groups. Throughout history, religious groups have found it ethical and moral to behead burn or otherwise sacrifice other humans for the benefit of their people and as a sacrifice to their gods. The Germans in the 1930s led by their dictator Adolph Hitler and the Nazi political party indicated that it was ethical to wipe out the Jewish race.

From the time of the birth of Christianity, the Christian religion and their followers have persecuted the Jews and the Jewish religion. From the time that I was a young boy, I knew about the persecution of Jews, but I never understood it. Growing up during the Second World War, one could not help but hear about the Holocaust. As a youngster, I often wondered why some White folk wanted to kill other White folk. Upon looking at them, I could not tell the difference between a Jew and another white person. I knew the reason that White people persecuted Blacks. It was about skin color and race. I did not understand that the persecution of Jews by Christians was about religion. Upon research, there appears to be a number of reasons given by Christians for this persecution of Jews:

> (1) Christians blame the Jewish race for the crucifixion of Jesus Christ, the person who the Christians call their 'Son of God'. The Christians labeled the Jews "Christ killers."

> (2) The Jewish people who resided within Christian countries refused to be converted to Christianity. The Jewish people were strong about their faith. The Christians were able to convert other conquered people to their religion. But throughout

history, they were unable to convert the Jews to Christianity. Many a Jew died rather than give up his faith.

(3) Christians also have accused Jews of kidnapping children to steal their blood for a Jewish ritual called 'Blood Libel'. In the Ritual, blood is required for use in the baking of bread used in the Jewish Passover ceremony.

(4) Jews, because they were excluded from many occupations in Christian countries, became successful money lenders which offended the Christian populations because the Jews charged interest on the money that they lent. Many Christians became indebted to Jews because of the lending practices. Often time, the Christian countries cancelled the Christian debts to Jews which amounted to stealing the Jews' money.

(5) The Jews were also accused of well poisoning. During the Black Death epidemic of the 14th Century, the Jews were accused of poisoning the wells of Europe which was attributed by many, at the time, as the cause of the Black Death. The Black Death—or The Plague, as it was sometimes referred to—caused the death of millions of Europeans. It was later learned that the Black Death was caused by fleas carried by rats.

(6) Host desecration was another offence that the Christians accused the Jews of being guilty of. Host desecration involved the mistreatment or malicious use of a consecrated Host, the sacred bread used in the Eucharistic service of the divine liturgy of the Christian Mass. Christians alleged that a piece of bread could be changed into the actual body of their Christ and be fed to Christians during the ceremonial Mass. Wine was also purported to be converted into the blood of Jesus Christ. A parishioner receiving the bread and wine was taught to believe that he had received the body and blood of Jesus Christ, The Son of God. Again, the Jews were alleged to have desecrated the bread. How the Jews were supposed to have gotten hold of the Hosts, I never found out.

So, I found out that the persecution of the Jews was about religion, not race. Most Jews are Caucasians. It was the Caucasian Christians who led the persecution of the Jews.

The above reasons were why the Christian faiths, both Catholic and Protestant, had for centuries persecuted the Jewish people who were of the Judaism faith. For centuries, Christians had murdered Jews, ran them out of European countries, confiscated their property and at times destroyed whole populations of Jews in different areas of Europe.

The Muslims faith was also not kind to the Jewish people. The Muslims committed the same kind of offences against the

Jews as was committed by the Christians. The Jews were originally in the lands around present day Palestine but were run out when the Muslims took over that part of the world. Jews then dispersed into Europe.

The above is a synopsis of a long and violent history of the persecution of Jews by Europeans. And then, along came Hitler. I would not consider Adolph Hitler a religious person. I take it for granted that he was a Christian. He was a politician who became a very powerful leader, implementing a genocidal agenda. He obliviously hated the Jews and their religion. The Jews had been a problem for the Christians for centuries. Christians had beaten them, run them off, burned them, stole their possessions and murdered whole groups of Jews. But they (Jews) were still around and faithful to their religion.

Hitler blamed the Jews for everything that he saw that was wrong with the world and indicated that he had an answer once and for all to the Jewish Problem. Hitler's "Final Solution" was to kill every Jew on earth which he deemed would be the ethical solution to the Christian-Jewish problem. He and his henchmen designed concentration camps, rounded up the Jews and sent them off to the death camps to be killed. It is estimated that 6,000,000 Jews were put to death as a result of Hitler's plan for a final solution to the Jewish problem.

During the time of programs against Judaism, the leaders of Catholic and Protestant Churches did not protest against the treatment of the Jews by the Germans or their policies and programs developed to exterminate the Jewish population. The results of the Holocaust—the slaughter of millions of people—evidenced the hatred of one religious group for another.

The Germans were not the only nationality involved in the Holocaust. In other European countries that were invaded and conquered by the Germans during World War II, the citizens of those countries participated in the round up and murder of the Jewish people in those countries. The overwhelming hatred of one religious group for another is a stain on the so-called mercifulness of the God claimed by the representatives of the religions guilty of the slaughter of the Jewish people.

Remember though, it cannot be blamed on a God because there is no God. The people on this earth who commit atrocities must accept the blame for the crimes they commit. If the all-loving and all-caring God existed that religious people proclaim Him to be, why would he allow the carnage and the violence that has existed in the world? Often times the people that have perpetrated the violence have done so in the name of their god.

Man has used every word in the written language to praise God. God is good. God is great. He is all loving. He is all powerful. God looks out for mankind. He is forgiving and merciful. God is benevolent. God is almighty. He is all knowing. God is Trustworthy. Trust in the Lord. Those are some of the praises given to God by his religious followers. If He is all that His believers say He is, would He allow His so-called creation (man) to suffer the things that men suffer?

Those who believe in God, whether they are Protestant, Catholic, Buddhist, Hindu, Muslim or any other religious faith, will advise their followers and anybody that they can address, to pray to their god for the solving of their problems. There have been many people throughout the world born with deformities. There have been tons of prayers said on behalf of those individuals. Unless medicine or science has developed cures for that segment of the world's population, those deformed individuals are still around.

Some religions have claimed miracles performed by God to cure some of the afflicted of their birth defects. That doesn't make sense. If a God exists that can perform miracles for some (a very few have been claimed) why doesn't He do it for all? If he is all powerful, why would he allow people to be born with afflictions at all? I overheard a preacher say that he had the power through god to heal people. And that he could lay hands on the person who was afflicted, and the person could get up out of the wheel chair after he (the preacher) touched him. The preacher was on television and there was no afflicted person with him. The preacher was asking for donations for his fraud appeal.

Praying to God and mediating to a God will protect us from evil. So say those who practice and believe in the existence of a God or Gods. There are still some religions that worship more than one God. Buddhism is a religion that has more than one God. If it is true that praying to God will protect one from evil, then why did God not protect the people around the world who from time to time have been massacred by the people of other religious faiths or the same religious faith? Did God take sides with the massacring against the massacred? The massacred prayed just as hard to their God as did those who caused their death.

In Elaine, Arkansas, in 1919, a group of Black sharecroppers were meeting in a church. The purpose of the meeting was to organize in an effort to protest for a fairer share of the profits that resulted from their labor. White farmers demanded an obscene percentage of the profits that Black labor produced.

Local white men knew about the meeting and came to the church—armed. They were determined to keep their power over Black people which was inherited from slavery and continued to dominate Black-White relations after the Civil War. They fired shots into the church. The Black men inside the church fired back and a white man was killed. White troops from a nearby military base and white vigilantes from town gathered in a mob and went on a rampage. Over 200 Black men, women and children were killed.[9]

Blacks and whites were both Christians and they prayed to and believed in the same god. If I believed in there being a God, I would say that God took the side of the White people in the above instance—and in all of the instances of bigotry practiced by white people against Blacks in America throughout history. But since I

---

[9] Wikipedia, "Elaine Race Riot."

don't believe in god, I say that bigotry is the result of man's evilness toward other men who are unlike themselves.

If there was a God with all of the superlatives that man gives to their God, my mind would not let me think that the God would allow such atrocious behavior. This God would fix man's mind to eliminate thoughts and behavior that are detrimental to His creations. But there is no God to control man's mind, to eliminate man's inhumanity towards other men. The only thing that stops man from committing more heinous acts toward his fellow man is his ability to look back upon the acts that he has committed and feel guilty about the horrendous deeds that he has performed or caused to be performed and in some cases has developed the ability to administer justice for crimes committed.

In some instances, man has also developed humane behavior to move life forward to make up for past wrongs. Although man has made progress on his own toward the humane treatment of his fellow man, I think that evilness will always remain in some men on Earth.

Natural Disasters, Religion and Questions about Man's Existence

Religious populations that live in areas of natural disasters pray to their God to protect them from nature's wrath. If it wasn't for man's ability to build stronger structures and to tame rivers and fire (somewhat) man would still be experiencing the tremendous catastrophic deaths from nature's calamities. No matter how much man prays to God, deaths will still occur because of nature's rearrangements of the earth.

Man has learned to limit deaths from natural disasters because of his increased mastering of engineering techniques. Praying to a God will not prevent an earthquake. If a quake is going to happen, it will happen. Man has developed the ability to know what causes earthquakes and to be better prepared when they do happen to limit the loss of life when the earth erupts. Floods, fire, hurricanes, tornados, and earthquakes are going to happen, and man cannot prevent them from happening no matter how hard he prays to a god.

Questions Concerning Man, His Existences, God and Religion

Since the beginning of man's existence, man has had queries about his existence and his relationship to God, his life and religion. Here are some questions that have perplexed man since his presence on earth.

- *Why Was Man Born and What Was (Is) Man's Purpose on Earth?*

Upon reviewing the history of man, it appears that the following are the reasons for man's existence

1. To pass on his genes to future generations
2. To use his intellect to improve the condition of man's life on earth
3. To develop cultures for the protection of man and to create laws that protect his relationship with other men

4. To continue to learn about the workings of the natural world in an effort to maximize the benefits that can be received from nature.

- *Is There Life After Death?*

No one knows. No one has come back from the dead and told us of an existence in death. There have been instances where humans were thought to be dead for a short period of time and then the person was ruled not to be dead. The death had been misdiagnosed.

The purported dead person, upon being revived, related some things that were experienced during the time they were supposedly dead. Some reported a kind of out of body experience. Some people grabbed on to the story told by the revived person as proof that life exists after death. Most people want to believe in the after-death experience, and they will grab at anything to bolster their faith.

I believe the person who was thought to be dead was dreaming. We all experience dreams when we sleep. The revived person was in a state of sleep and was dreaming about the incidents that he was relating. Death is a subject that has to interest us all. At some point in our existence we will all find out about death when we die.

- *Can a Person Lead a Good Life Without Religion?*

Yes, one can. Every culture has laws, ethics and values. If a person follows those indices they will most often enjoy and get to pursue the delights of a full life. Although, most often, people who are religious are involved in setting the values of a culture, those values emanate from what those involved think is best for the culture. If the person in the culture does not believe in the religion of the culture, they can respect those who do and hope that their nonbelief will also be respected. There have been cultures wherein non-believers in the culture have been put to death. Nothing is guaranteed in life. You can practice religion or not. You still can be struck by a car or get caught up in a manmade calamity such as war or be stricken with a death inducing illness whether you are religious or not.

- *Do I Have to Pray and Honor a God?*

There are over 4,000 religions in the world and they all praise and honor various Gods. Some religions still have multiple gods. All religions boast that their god is the true god. If one lives in an eastern culture, they do not honor the same god that is honored in the jungles of Brazil. If you have to pray to a God to make you feel better and more secure, by all means pray to some god. But your life can exist without prayer because I firmly believe God does not exist.

- *Is There a One True Religion and a One and Only God?*

Not according to man. A religion is a particular system of faith and worship. Each religion espouses that their path to their god(s) is the only true path to salvation. There are many religions to choose from. Most Religions do have values and ethics that they believe in. If one needed to join a group of like-minded people and were looking for a religion to join, I would recommend that they choose one that mirrors the values that they have for themselves. As far as a god to choose from I couldn't make a recommendation because god is a confusing concept that is inconceivable to me. As I said before, there are so many gods that are recognized by men around the world, if one had to choose a god, one should join a group the has a god that will satisfy the values of the person making the choice.

- *Many Men Profess That There Is a God. Should I Go Along and Believe with Them?*

To say that there is a God is to say that one has the complete knowledge of the mysteries of life. To the point that we now exist in, no one has enough knowledge to be certain that there is a God. Man is ever increasing his knowledge of the universe and as time progresses, man's comprehension of life increases. There was a time when man thought that the cure for many illnesses was tied to some conjuring ceremony to some God or Goddess. Advances in man's knowledge of medicine have eliminated those ritual witchcraft kinds of practices.

People are free to choose to believe in God and to follow other men, who advocate the belief in god, as they want to. But most men who believe in a god will admit that their beliefs are based in **faith** not facts.

- *I Have Been Told That If I Follow the Christian 10 Commandments, I Will Have a Good Life. Is That True?*

The first 5 Commandments of the 10 commandments are religious.

1. Thou shall have no other gods before me
2. Thou shall not make unto thee any graven image
3. Thou shall not take the name of the Lord thy God in vain
4. Remember the Sabbath day. Keep it holy.
5. Honor thy father and thy mother

The five commandments listed above are religious in nature. If you did not obey those first 4 and if there is no God, there could be no effect on your life. The fifth commandment does not always apply to an individual. I was given up at birth and never knew who my father was. I could not honor him if I had wanted to.

The last 5 Commandments of the 10 Commandments could refer to societies' laws.

6. Thou shall not kill
7. Thou shall not committee adultery
8. Thou shall not steal
9. Thou shall not bear false witness against thy neighbor

10. Thou shall not covet thy neighbor's wife

Commandments 6, 8 and 9 are definitely Commandments that address the laws of a society and are punishable by sanctions if committed. The commandments against adultery and coveting thy neighbor's wife (or husband) could be religious or secular law depending upon which society one lives in. In the western culture, I have not heard of a woman going to jail if she spends the afternoon having sex, in a hotel with another woman's husband unless some other violations are involved.

There are other countries where religious laws have been incorporated into the legal laws of the country. In some Arabic countries where the Muslim faith is practiced, it is against the legal system for a woman to go bareheaded or for women to wear a bikini. Those laws are religious in nature, as opposed to common sense laws against killing or lying. A society would be destroyed if there were no laws against doing bodily harm to one another and some kind of punishment for those who commit those infractions. The world would survive if a woman lets her hair down or she was seen with her body half exposed in a swim suit as happens every day in Western cultures. Men grin and bear it— seeing the beauty of a woman. There were cultures whereby men have had more than one wife. Those cultures obviously didn't relate to the 10 Commandments.

- *How Does Sin Affect My Life?*

Sin is a religious concept. The law is a civil concept. If you break a civil law, you could be accountable for a civil sanction. If you believe in a religion and break a religious law, the consequence is whatever you believe, in your mind will happen, as a result of one being indoctrinated by that religion. If you believe in that religion, then you are going to believe that you are going to be affected by the tenets of the religion.

As an example, in Christianity, Catholics teach, that if you have thoughts about having sex with another human outside of marriage, they say those are improper thoughts and it is immoral for you to do so. By the standards of that religion, you have committed a sin. If you are not a Christian and you don't believe in god, you can have all of the sexual thoughts that come into your head as long as you do not act in an unlawful way toward other humans.

In Christianity, they say that sin is inherent in God's creation. The religion says that no one can escape the fires of hell unless one takes refuge in God and obeys his laws. That religion says, one cannot avoid sin. Christians indicate that everyone is born with sin. According to Christians, all men inherited sin from Adam and Eve when they disobeyed the edict from God to refrain from eating the so-called fruit of knowledge in the Garden of Eden.

The Buddhist religion indicates that the idea of sin or original sin has no place in Buddhism.

There is also no concept of original sin in Hinduism. Sin may arise from disobedience to god's law. According to Hindu beliefs, most sin leads to sickness or disease either in the present birth or in future rebirths. Being born again, or reincarnation, is a major tenet of Hinduism.

- *Do Hell and the Devil Really Exist?*

I hope the hell not! Remember, earlier we said that we don't know if life after death exists. In order for Hell to be a reality, there would have to be life after death. For many people on earth, Hell exists while they are alive. People who existed in slavery, humans that are deformed, mankind that experiences war up close and personnel, persons that do not get enough to eat and people who go through life under torturous conditions are experiencing Hell-like conditions while alive.

The concept of hell in Christianity is supposed to be where people spend an eternity for unforgiven transgressions against God. God was supposed to have created Hell when he expelled his rebellious angels from heaven. God is supposed to have created the devil who reigns over Hell and the devil desires equality with god, so they are adversaries. If god is all powerful and the creator and the destroyer of all things, why doesn't he get rid of the devil? If god created man and he is purported to have love for his creations, why would he create a trap for his creations that would lead to so called eternal damnation.

Remember, earlier, we said that God was created by man. The earliest writers who wrote the old and new testament were the creators of the concept of the one God theory. They gave this God, whom they created, responsibility for all the positive things that happened to man. The writers realized that there was a problem with this concept. Because if this God was responsible for everything that happened to man, he also had to be responsible for all of the bad things that happen to man. Thus, there was a contradiction about God's goodness that had been built into the story line about God. Man had to come up with a being to own responsibility for the bad behavior of man and for the merciless things that happen to God's creation—man. As we said earlier the writers invented the Devil.

Even though the writers had invented God as being all powerful, which meant that he should have easily been able to defeat the devil, if there was a devil, they (the writers of the Old and New Testament) stuck with the story line about the existence of the Devil which was an inconsistency about the omnipotence of the God that they had created. The writers' audiences (religions) overlooked and bought into the writing flaws of the writers because they were eager to accept a flawless God. They were eager to have blame for man's transgressions placed on another being, even though God created that being. The devil had been one of Gods top angels who had become rebellious against him—so goes the story of the devil's creation.

There are conflicting opinions about the devil and Hell in the Hindu and Buddhist religion, but the idea of eternal damnation is impossible within those religions because of their reincarnation theory. According to the Hindu and Buddhist religion, hell might be a stopover place until the being is reincarnated.

The Islam religion believes that there is a hell but does not believe that Hell is eternal. The Quran (The Muslim Holy Book)

101:9-10 states that "like a fetus goes through the stages of physical maturation in a mother's womb, a guilty soul passes through the stages of spiritual maturation in hell until they are cleansed." Hell, in Islam, is therefore a penitentiary and is not a permanent place as is in Christianity. If I believed in a hell, I would choose the Muslim version of a temporary place to cleanse myself so that I could get out of the fires of hell at some point.

The writers of the Muslim religion (in the Quran) allowed their sinful followers to have some hope for redemption after death. Theirs is a better more appealing story. If I wanted to believe in a religious interpretation of hell, I would choose Islam based on their belief in hell and giving me a second chance at life after death. But I understand that their revelation is just a story. A different twist on the story told about hell from the Christian religion perspective.

- *Do Miracles Still Happen?*

Miracles are defined as a divine operation that transcends what is normally perceived as the natural law. If a person could look at a building and will the building to raise that would be a miracle. It cannot be explained upon any natural basis.

There have been miracles reported in religion. Most miracles have been reported in the Christian faith. Some of the supposed miracles are:

The Creation activity by the spoken word of God. He merely spoke and it was done (Hebrew 11:3)

Jesus walked on water of the lake (Acts 3:1-10)

Lazarus was dead for 4 days, then he was raised by Jesus (John 11:1-45)

Christ multiplying loaves and fishes to feed the multitude. (Mathew 14:13-21)

The above were reported as miracles that happened during the time that Jesus Christ was alive, which was in the first century. He (Christ) was also reported to have risen from the dead after his death. That would also qualify as a miracle. In the early days of Christianity there seems to have been many miracles reported. Christ's apostles were given credit in the Bible for miracles that they were supposed to have performed. The apostles were men who traveled with Christ while He preached and converted men to the Christian faith. Those men were credited with not only bringing forth the Christian religion after Christ died but also performing miracles.

Ancient man's gods, before Christianity, received recognition for performing miracles. There are other sets of men and woman who have been reported to have been given prestige for bringing about miracles. We wrote about this group when we earlier wrote of the saints.

In order to become a saint, according to the Catholic Church, one had to be credited with two miracles. To the best of my knowledge, most of the miracles credited to the saints have been miracles that involved the candidate for sainthood curing someone who was ill. The ill person prayed to the saint candidate and the person got cured. The cure was supposed to happen because of the intervention of the person who the faithful was trying to canonize.

Canonization is when the Catholic Church officially declares a dead person to be a saint. As a young person growing up in the Catholic religion, I was taught that there is usually a specific purpose connected to a miracle. I was taught that the religion believes that miracles are works of God, either directly or through the prayers and intersessions of a specific saint or saints. Another example of a miracle, as proclaimed by the Catholic Church, would be the conversion of a person or a group of persons to the Catholic faith.

There used to be numerous claims of miracles in the Catholic Church but now that man has the ability to scientifically test miracle claims, the number of claimed miracles have dropped off. I don't believe in miracles, but if there were miracles performed by a god, it would seem unfair for the God to favor, with a cure for some people by a miracle and let other people suffer with their medical illness.

I asked a Catholic priest "why are there now so few miracles reported?" He answered, "A number of the miracles were performed when the church was being established. Now, that the church is established there is no need for as many miracles. Too many miracles would take away the force and influence of prior miracles." His answer leads me to believe that he was saying that miracles can be turned on and off at will. I told him that there are still people in need of miracles so he should advise the church elders to start up the miracle machine–if he can.

Recently the Catholic Church wanted to declare a recently deceased Pope as a saint. A pope is the head of the Catholic Church. Pope John Paul was given credit for a miracle when a catholic nun, Sister Marie-Pierre recovered from Parkinson's disease. She had prayed to the deceased Pope for recovery from the Illness

If I believed in miracles, I would ask to be alive and healthy until I was 120 years old. We would see what would happen to that request.

- *Will Religion Help Me If and When I Experience Suffering?*

There are two kinds of sufferings, physical and mental. Physical suffering can result from an illness or from an accident that occurs to our body. Suffering from pain that results from an accident, can in many cases be relieved by modern medicine and modern surgical techniques. With the advances being made in health care, applying medical techniques can even alleviate some deformities that some men are born with. There still are instances of physical sufferings that man might want to call on a God or some supernatural being for help – like being trapped in a burning automobile. In desperation, one can pray to god or any other imaginary creature to see if one can get lucky enough to have someone appear to pull him out of a predicament so that he can avoid the sufferings. Unfortunately, it seems there are times that occur in man's life when man is incapable of avoiding circumstances that will bring about sufferings that will lead to death.

Man has learned to relieve other men of physical pain even in the throes of death. People, who are at the end of their life, when body functions have broken down, do not have to endure the pain and suffering that once was the fate of some persons leaving the earthly sphere. Hospice care is now available to relieve the suffering of death. Drugs are administered to relieve the pain and suffering that were associated with the coming of death.

Mental suffering can result from a number of causes: hunger, fear, the loss of loved ones, war, safety concerns etc. Islam like other religions recommends that you pray to their God, Allah, to help you in the time of your mental sufferings. In Islam, the religion states that the faithful must endure sufferings with faith and hope and not resist or ask why. Accept suffering as it is Allah's will. So says the Muslim faith. When people suffer it makes them think of Allah. Suffering is the time to find Allah and value faith while doing so, is a tenet of the Islamic religion.

Persons who are suffering from mental causes can best rely on people in society that are specialist who are trained to deal with problems that cause mental sufferings. If one is not capable of alleviating their mental suffering on their own, they should seek out those individuals who have some expertise in solving their kind of problems. The persons sought can be counselors, government officials, medical personnel and even people who have no professional experience but have a religious affiliation.

Advice from religious people might be valuable if one can separate the solution from the god-intervention. Even better, people need to try and develop the ability to alleviate the mental suffering, in their life, on their own. If one searches hard enough and has faith in their own ability to find solutions, they might be able to find resolutions to their mental sufferings.

- *Is It Better to Raise Children in a Religious Environment?*

If you want to raise your children in a mystical realm rather than have them use reason, then you should raise them with a religious foundation. Most of the world chooses to do that because most of the world is religious to some extent.

But one can raise a child using ethics and common sense to produce an offspring that abides by what is good for mankind. Moral principles can be taught and instilled by non-religious parents to their children minus—the influence of a supernatural being. Children need to be raised to emulate their parents' ethical and moral behavior and to use judgement as they come into maturity. Children need to to taught love, respect, discipline, structure, ethics and consequence. Those values can be instilled in children without the fear of a supernatural being.

- *Do All Religions Have a God?*

There is at least one major religion that does not rely on a deity. That religion is Confucianism. Confucianism is a religion where a supernatural being is somewhat in the religion, but the deity is not the focal point of worship. Confucianism is defined as a system of education, ethics and statesmanship taught by Confucius and his disciples, stressing love for humanity, ancestor worship, reverence for parents and harmony in thought and conduct.[10]

Confucianism originated in China. There are people who question whether Confucianism is a religion. There is no God honored in this creed, as there is a supernatural being who is present in most other religions.

The religion was started about 500 years before the Christ of Christianity was born. Confucius, the founder of the religion, regarded himself as a teacher not a god. He regarded himself as a transmitter of ancient truths rather than an inventor of new ones. His instructions were aimed at character building and self-cultivation. He taught through conversation and posing provocative questions. Confucius was a normal mortal man. He liked to fish, hunt, sing, enjoyed the arts and he enjoyed good drink and food. Confucius' name is one of a few names that are recognized in recorded history.[11]

Some people think of Confucianism as a philosophy and not a religion. Confucianism does have temples (churches) but no formal headquarters such as the Catholic Church's Vatican that.

The central ethical principle of Confucianism is embodied by a statement credited to Confucius. "Do not do to others what

---

[10] Dictionary.com, "Confucianism"
[11] Stephen Prothero, *God Is Not One* (Harper Collins, 2010) pp 101-130

you do not want done to yourself." The family is the center of the religion and comes before the individual. God is not a core concern in Confucianism. Confucianism is concerned about how to live your life properly, to be a good person, to serve your family and your nation. Character building is one of the core values of the religion. Learning, hard work and family reverence are the fundamentals of the conviction. All of the above can be achieved without the reliance on, or the prostrating to, a god figure. Confucianism pushes man to develop and rely on himself to improve his and others' lives.

Confucians value industrious persons, thriftiness, family, loyalty, duty and respect for authority. Other religions advocate those values, but they rely on a God or supernatural being to intercede on behalf of the worshiper to attain those standards. Confucianism stresses how to live now, not in the afterlife.

Social life is essential to Confucians. Attention should be focused on social matters and living in the here and now. Confucius was not interested in religious salvation and the afterlife. Instead of worshipping a god, the religion was meant to build character to be used to improve man's interaction with other men. In this religion there is a lack of interest in the divine but a focus on human flourishing. There is no preoccupation with gods and with life after death.

Confucianism is an authority directed religion. Its emphasis is on ritualized behavior which is to say that manners, etiquette and even body language toward each other and the government are important in this religion. Being considerate of others is central to Confucianism; rituals are serious: rulers over subjects, father over sons, husband over wives.

The religion from time to time, in past centuries has been the official State religion for the Governments of China. The Chinese communist party thought of integrating communism and Confucianism because of the rigid ideology, customs, culture and habits of the religion but the merger between the Government and the religion did not happen with the Communist this time. Although the Communist Party flirted with Confucianism, in the end the Communists found it hard to associate with anything that was remotely coupled with a god.

Confucianism in some respects is a fixed and unchanged religion, but the possibility exists that the religion can be transformed into delving into science, technology, liberalism and democracy. Other religions have changed their philosophies and practices over the years. To some extent, one of the most conservative of religions, the Catholic Church has changed and become more in tune with the modern world. The Church now allows the Mass to be said in the native language of the country wherein the Mass is being held - instead of in Latin as it used to be said.

Confucianism is a religion that has always concentrated on the development of man without the reliance on spiritual beings becoming involved in the maturation and the advancement of achieving human –heartedness.

If I were a person seeking a religion, I would investigate and be drawn to this religion because it avoids the dependence on a mystical being and recommends that men can and should seek harmony with each other. The inflexibility of the religion could be addressed to deal with the changing times so that its philosophy could deal with the changing needs of mankind to work out the world's problems without the spiritual interference that burdens other religions.

- *What Does the Televangelist Bring to Religion?*

In the 1920s, man learned to send communications over the air. As a result of this capability news, theatre, fictional reading and religious programs were available to be heard by masses of people around the world. The media in which this communication took place was radio.

Religious leaders now had the ability to connect with a wider audience to preach their version of Christianity or any other religion that they espoused. The preachers took to the air ways and religious programs became a staple along with comedy, music, crime, cowboy and adventure programs.

Radio broadcasts were seen as a complementary activity to the missionary practice of sending the message of Christianity to the faithful and to convert more of the population to the belief in God.

Two of the most famous preacher pioneers on the radio in the 1930s and 1940s was Charles Coughlin and Bishop Fulton J.

Sheen. They were both Catholic; Coughlin was also a Catholic priest.

Charles Coughlin was a fervent anti-communist. In the decade prior to his radio broadcasts, the Communists had taken over Russia and the Communist Manifesto was being pushed worldwide. Father Coughlin (as he was called) mixed politics and religion and riled against Communism as he passed the message of God to his listeners. Communism is a godless philosophy. The priest spent a large amount of his broadcast time, associating the devil with Marxism. Father Coughlin was also considered an anti-Semite. In the '30s and early '40s being outspoken against Jews did not carry the stigma that it does today. That was the time of Hitler in Germany and there was more of an open bias against Jews in the world.

Fulton J Sheen was a Catholic Bishop who began with a radio program preaching about God in the 1940s. He switched his message to television in the 1950s. He was a very popular radio/television minister and he was the inspiration for many of the televangelist who followed him in later decades.

In the 1950s, television surpassed the radio as the instrument for communication in American. Religious ministers took to the television media to deliver their messages concerning God. Televangelists became very popular because their followers or potential followers could sit back in the comfort of their home and absorb a sermon about the goodness of god and be instructed in the ways they could relate to the Supreme Being.

The televangelists reached and still reach millions of people through their broadcasts. The messages that they send appear to have the following component parts:

- They tell their people that God is present in their life and that God will help them if they recognize God and ask for his help
- The preachers promote self-improvement goals for their people
- The ministers caution their followers that the Devil is working against everything that they do
- The Christian ministers instruct their followers to call on Jesus when hard times are experienced
- They ask for money

I have listened to a number of televangelist programs and I have no problem with the preachers promoting self-improvement behaviors for their listeners. They tell their flock to "have a positive expectation about their lives, something good will happen for them if they work to improve their status in life." They also preach to the congregation to let go of bad behavior and to be positive about friends and relatives. "Be of help and assistance, when you can, to your fellow man" is advice that the televangelists preach to their television audience.

I am in agreement with most of the above messages accept when the preachers tie those behaviors to a God. They are saying that man is incapable of improving unless his improvement is tied to a supernatural being. Man has been responsible for his

improvements and his calamities since his existences on earth.
Since his presences in life, man has created and discarded a
number of gods which he glorified and sought advice from. But
most men will not believe or understand that man is responsible
for his life without Christ or Allah or the hundreds of other gods
that man has worshipped throughout his existence.

I don't fault the televangelists for the one major thing that
some accuse them of, being money grubbing frauds. I look at
them as providing entertainment for those who enjoy that kind of
showmanship. Entertainment costs and televangelists have to
raise money to stay on the air. Air personalities have to earn a
living and if that's what they do and they provide enjoyment for
their television congregation, then so be it, that they raise money.

But, one of their own has given a scathing rebuke of the
televangelist community in a series of articles. John McArthur, an
American pastor and President of Master's University and
Seminary, renowned for his internationally syndicated Christian
program *Grace To You*, wrote articles highly critical of some
televangelists who purported to preach the gospel. The following
is an excerpt from one of the articles written by Mr. McArthur:

"Someone needs to say this plainly. Faith healers and
health and wealth preachers who dominate religious
television are shameless frauds. Their message is not the
true gospel of Jesus Christ. There is nothing spiritual or
miraculous about their on-stage chicanery. It is all a
devious ruse designed to take advantage of desperate
people. They are not godly ministers but greedy imposters

who corrupt the Word of God for money's sake. They are not real pastors who shepherd the flock of God but hirelings whose only design is to fleece the sheep. Their love of money is glaringly obvious in what they say, as well as how they live. They claim to possess great spiritual power, but in reality, they are rank materialists and enemies of everything holy."[12]

Well, one of their own said that they were frauds. As I said before, I think that they are entertainers. Providing what their audience wants to hear is worth some remittance from the spectators who thirst for the programs.

There are programs on television that talk about ghosts and the living dead and we have our modern versions of Superman. Those are entertainment programs that sponsors are willing to pay for so that their product can be advertised over the air.

I don't think that there are many commercially sponsored televangelist programs. In order for the televangelists to be on the airways they must get the people who enjoy the programming to pay for the privilege of seeing and hearing them. There are millions of people in the world who believe in God and want the programs to continue. Therefore, let them have their entertainment and let them pay for it. And let the preachers continue their lifestyles. Other fantasy entertainment stars also become rich and famous. Why not the televangelist?

---

[12] "A Colossal Fraud" (Code A391), *Grace to You*, 7 December 2009.

Remember, though, the god that they pitch doesn't exist. The parts of their program that promote self-help should be good for their audiences, though.

Human Intellect, Creativity, and Curiosity

Humans surely don't understand all there is to be known about life. And they surely don't know anything about death other than that everybody dies. Over the millions of years that man has been in existence man has increased his knowledge about the existence of life. The body has been studied and the brain has been dissected and examined. We now have a good idea how the body and the brain function. We have discovered how different parts of the brain control different physical and mental functions of our body. The functioning of the heart, lungs, kidneys, blood and all major organs are understood. The knowledge of how those body parts work and their makeup has allowed man to repair them and to use that skill to prolong the life of man. There was a time when life expectancy for the average man was maybe between 40 and 50 years. Today, it is in the 70s, at least.

Mentally, man is now in better control of the thinking capacity of his life. We are better able to make decisions that benefit humanity. We are still capable of doing destructive things that are harmful to the human race, but man's discovery of material uses of natural resources coupled with the better understanding of human needs has tremendously improved man's comfort level in life. Man's discoveries of the use of 'ideas and materials' to make life better were realized by man using his own intellect, creativity and curiosity. Man did not have god sitting beside him and showing him the way when electricity was invented. Man produced that invention on his own. It was a life changing discovery which has benefitted and made life more livable for most, if not all of life on the planet. Man has consistently improved his standard of living since the beginning of his presence on earth. He has learned to use fire to cook with which has improved his body. Cooked food killed bacteria that were harmful to man.

There are those who say that man has advanced with the help of god. Which god are you talking about—the Christian god or the god who was worshipped in China at least a century before the Christian god was created?

Paper is one of the inventions that has given man the ability to put things in writing which has allowed him to carry ideas forward so that other men could build on those ideas and add to the improvement of life. In China, where paper was invented, the gods of Buddhism and Taoism were worshipped at the time. Christianity was not yet born.

When the present-day Christians tell me that god was responsible for the invention of things to make life more bearable, they are crediting the god of the Chinese with inspiring that invention (paper) because it was discovered in China at least 100 years before Christ and the Christian religion was born. Thus, it is a contradiction for Christians to say that god inspired that invention because the Christians do not recognize the faiths honored in China as the true religion and the Christians believe that the gods of those religions are false gods. The Buddhist and the Taoist say the same thing about the Christian god.

In actually, no god was involved in the discovery of paper nor has any god been involved in any of the numerous things that man has discovered in nature to either improve life or to jeopardize man's existence on earth. The following are some of man's inventions that have improved his life or have potential for his destruction.

- Gun powder—Destructive potential
- Penicillin—Life saving
- Rockets—Destructive potential
- Nuclear fission—Destructive potential
- Personnel Computers—Expanded human capabilities
- Air plane—Brought the world closer together
- Telephone—Revolutionized our ability to communicate
- Electricity—Its use has reshaped our way of life
- Printing Press—Revolutionized the spread of knowledge
- Compass—Navigational devise has been a major force in human exploration
- Plow—Allowed man to increase agricultural productivity

The above are a small sample of man's creativity. These were man's inventions. Man was born with the capacity to creatively look at the world which surrounds him and to image how he can change his environment to better serve his life. Over time he has accomplished many world changing challenges. But it was slow going.

Collaterally, man was quick to imagine the concept of god. That concept has been with man since the beginning of his existence. But slowly, and surely over millions of years, man has also changed his environment to better suite his needs. Maybe, man quickly created a god because he was slow to understand and make changes to his environment. Historians trace man's existence back for millions of years. Yet, it has been in a relatively short period of time that man has made tremendous leaps in using things in nature to advance civilization. It appears that one discovery accelerated the process for other discoveries. As man gains in knowledge of his environment there will be less of a need for the imagined intervention of a supernatural being.

Death

Death remains as the biggest mystery in man's life. Religions have promoted the thought that there is life after death. Is there some kind of existence after life? Death and god have been speculated on since man was aware of his existence. I have thought about my own death and I think that when I die, it is over. Some people that I have talked to speculate that death is a transition going from one existence to another. I think that my body will lie in the ground where it will rot. There will be no consciousness floating around, waiting for an adjudication day arrives when I will be judged for the things that I did in life.

That is a philosophy not shared by many people. It is a minority view. Many people believe that their life will be resurrected, and they will face that judgment day. Some believe that they will go straight to what they call Heaven because they indicate that they have led a good life and they will be rewarded with eternal bliss in a paradise.

I never met anyone that says that they are going to hell. I guess the bad actors think that they will be forgiven for their actions. Heaven and hell are the places that are envisioned by most people as a place to reside in after death. Earlier, we examined the concept of heaven and hell and concluded that these places are part of the mystic invention of religion. Religions have indoctrinated their followers to believe in those concepts.

As mentioned before, I have asked people what they think about the specifics of death and everybody that I have talked to tells me that they believe in some kind of life after their bodily life on earth is over. But besides floating around and waiting for the judgement day scenario, they can't explain what life is like after death. I don't fault them. They can't know what life is like after death. No one has come back and laid it out.

I sure hope that after I die there is no more life. Life on earth was (is) so damn stressful. I don't want any more life after I die. I had enough tension, trauma and anxiety for one life.

I am not alone with dealing with life's pressures. We have all dealt with the stresses in life and many people have had success dealing with a full life cycle. There are also people who have succumbed to life's trials and did not get to live a full life. People are killed in war, are murdered, die in natural disasters, succumb to diseases, starve to death, are massacred and some are stillborn.

I suspect that many of those people in the above categories, if they could, would wish that all that they had to deal with would be the comparatively small amount of stress that I have experienced. Their level of stress killed them, and they did not get to live a full life.

I have been lucky and have survived these stresses in my life:

- Abandoned at birth and becoming a ward of the State
- Raised in a cruel foster home
- Running from home and the police as a youngster
- Surviving four years in a Boys Home
- Staying alive in the Army
- Being a parent
- Working to keep a marriage together
- Lying to women for sex
- Earning two college degrees
- Working for 12 employers
- Surviving two bouts of cancer, a heart attack and a gunshot wound
- Contending with bodily changes in advanced age

- Avoiding highway accidents
- Avoiding being mugged in the streets
- Worrying about economic security

The above have been enough of a life time challenge for one life and it isn't yet over. I am bound to face other challenges as my time on earth draws near. Mind you, I am not complaining, I don't want to end my life before its time. I am just reminding the reader how it is and how I don't want another life after this life is over. I have been successful in dealing with the normal stresses that I have encountered in a life time. I am not suicidal. Thus far, I have navigated the good and the bad in life, the same as most other people. The only difference between me and those other people is when this life is over, I don't want another life. When I die, let me Rest in Peace.

Whose Side is God On?

Is there or isn't there a God? I know that I am out-voted when I say that there is no god. Millions, if not billions of people, say that there is a god. One proof (among many) that the god believers point to is the celestial bodies in the sky and earth in particular. As part of their proof they indicate that man is still discovering facts about the universe which justifies their faith in a Supreme Being who they say is responsible for the cosmos as well as everything else that man has encountered on Earth, as well as for man himself. If this supposedly to almighty god is real; does he take sides in human affairs?

God has caught the imagination of man and man is not about to let it go under any circumstances. Recently, I was watching television and was tuned to a program where the survivor of a mass shooting was being interviewed. A racist White man had entered into a church in one of the southern United States and shot and killed a number of the congregation. The incident happened in 2017. The survivor that was being interviewed, who had received a gunshot womb but survived the attack, was relating how during the assault she saw Jesus and that Jesus protected her from any further assault by the gunman. She was thanking her Lord for coming to her rescue during the incident. She indicated the Jesus had insured that she survived. I could tell by the woman's countenance that she was sincere and that she really believed that god had intervened to save her life.

As I watched the program, I wish that I would have had the opportunity to ask the lady some questions about her survival of the incident:

1. You all were worshiping God at the time of the incident. Why do you think that God picked you to live and let the others die?

2. This incident happened in a church where the people were gathered to do their God's work and to praise their Lord. Why did He (God) allow people to die in His House, in His place of worship?

3. Why did God allow this racist to walk into that church and commit this horrendous act in the first place?

That racist probably believed in God also, and it is not hard to reason that the racist in some way or the other thought that he was doing God's work.

The first question of why she alone was spared from destruction relates to the bigger universal question of why God seems to take sides in the protection of some men, and favor one man over another. Why does their God allow some to survive while others to die? Again and again we come across this question in relation to God singling out who will be saved and who will die. In the above case the preacher and a couple of the parishioners were killed. Were they less worthy than this woman to be protected from death by their God? They were gathered to do good works in the church. I don't know anything about the private lives of the people that were killed with the exception that the preacher was also an elected politician. But evidently according to the woman's story, Jesus only intervened in saving her life and let the others die.

On second thought it would not do any good to question the woman about the reason why she was spared and the others were not. She could not supply the answer. She might answer as many have answered in similar situations: "It was God's will that I survived."

I would give the following answer to my question. I would say that one evil-minded racist invaded their church and killed as many people as he could. He left that church with the thought that he had killed them all. The woman was shot but not fatally and survived the shooting. She was **lucky** as are all who survive being shot and live. I am carrying a bullet in my stomach that I received in 1975. I, too, am **lucky** that the perpetrator did not hit a vital organ. The reason why we are both alive is that we are lucky.

I don't know for sure, but the racist was probably a Christian. Christians believe in the same God. If so, this person who walked into the church and shot the people was a Christian who thought that God was on his side. His God is the same God that the woman he shot prays to. If this is the case, then the God that they both pray to and love took the side of the racist and allowed the racist to kill and wound the people in the church.

God had nothing to do with this case. There are evil men and women in the world, and they will do harm to other people based on their evilness no matter what their religious beliefs are. In this case, the evil man was a White man, pent on doing harm to Black people. There are also evil Black men, pent on doing harm to people of their own race or to other races. Evilness among men and women has existed since the world has existed. In China, Russia, Japan, Angola, Argentina and everywhere in the world there are people who take other people's lives. Good people—and bad people—have been the victims of man's wickedness. There has been no god to intervene to stop people from killing people.

Christians kill other Christians. Muslims kill other Muslims, and Hindus take the life of people in their religion. Since there is no god, there is no god to protect man from other men or to take sides. When wars are fought between men, the side that wins is the side that has the greater manpower or the greater tactical weapons.

- *Does Praying to a God Reap Rewards?*

I have heard many preachers tell their flock to love God and pray to Him and they shall be rewarded by God. I have no way of knowing how many people receive what they pray for, nor do I know how many people don't get what they pray for. Many people are going to pray. They have been trained throughout their life that if they pray to God, their prayers will be answered. Both good people and bad people say their prayers. It's not inconceivable to think that bad people who have committed murder will pray to God not to get caught. I have even heard of people praying for the demise of other people. There are voluminous things that one can pray for, such as:

- Having a baby
- Good health
- Getting a job
- Getting a raise
- A cure for illness
- A new love
- A promotion
- A new car

- Long life
- A winning sport team
- Good grades
- A nice home
- Acceptability
- A safe trip
- Successful children
- A successful marriage
- Vacation travel
- The demise of other people
- Success at thievery

These are only some of the things that people prayed for. The question is: did prayer help them achieve what they prayed for? And if received, how do we know it was the result of prayer?

I don't pray to a God for things that I want and that I need. I wish for or have wished for many of the above listed items. I have worked hard to put myself in a position to accomplish or process many of the things that I have wished for. Effort, hard work and luck have allowed me to be successful in receiving, **most**—not all—of the things that I desired.

Yes, I said **luck**. I have been lucky in life to come along at a time when a Black man could achieve a level of success that Black men could not achieve in prior generations. If I had been born in 1839 instead of 1939, I would have most probably been a slave. But being born in 1939 allowed me to live at a time when Black men were free. When I came out of college, it was in the era of Civil Rights and affirmative action. I was hired in a management position in corporate America which could not have happened if I had been born in a prior generation. Luck and preparation got me what I wanted.

I worked hard to get a college degree—to prepare myself so that I could accomplish my wish or hope to earn an income and to have had a good life. I was lucky enough to be in the right place at the right time to have my wish fulfilled. I didn't have money to attend college, but I was able to I attend college, junior college tuition-free. I got straight A's, in junior college so after graduation I was eligible and won a scholarship to a four-year institution—all expenses paid. When employed, I worked for a business that paid its employee's tuition reimbursement. After I got my master's degree, the company eliminated the program. I put in the hard work and was lucky enough to be in the program at the right time before it was eliminated.

I have contended that there is no God. So, if there is no God, people are praying to a supernatural being that does not exist. If they receive what they pray for it is because they have put effort into accomplishing the thing that they were (are) praying for. And the timing has been right for the thing to come to fruition. They think that their prayers are being answered, but it is the combination of preparation and luck that determines their victories.

When the religious person's prayers are not answered, what do they think has happened? There have been many religious persons who are known to say that their prayers went unanswered. In my estimation they did not understand that in order to receive what they were praying for they had to be an active participant in what they were trying to receive. If one just prays and sits back and waits for the prayer to be answered what they are trying to receive will not come—unless they are very lucky. A person has to be an active participant.

Just praying could have the effect of relieving the person of the need to take active measures to get what they want. People can also sometimes work their butt off and not get what they worked or wished for. Those people just were unlucky in their efforts. You can be unlucky and be a passenger on an airplane that crashes, or be drafted in a time of war and get killed in that war, or step out in front of a speeding automobile and get killed. Luck plays a part in life—good luck and bad luck.

I surmise that most of the people who go to gambling casinos in the United States are religious and I would suffice it to say that those people say a prayer to their God before they enter the gambling place. They probably ask their God to make them a winner. We know that the overwhelming number of people who go to the casinos lose their money. How do these people reconcile that God never answered their prayer to be winners? So, God is not answering the players' prayers? The players don't know it but there is no god to answer their prayers. People who win money are doing so because they become lucky with the turn of the slots or they might have skill at some particular card game that allows them to win.

I think that in life, one can pray all that they want to in order to achieve what they want but they must contribute effort to achieve what they are praying for. If the effort is sufficient and other factors that cannot be controlled by the prayer fall in line, they have a good chance of having their hopes become a reality.

The Creation of the Earth and Mankind

I have made an argument against the concept of there being a god. I know many people will dispute the argument against there being a supreme being. Although, Atheists are a minority, there are other Atheists that have also made the written argument against there being a god. Those fellow atheists have probably done a better job than me. I haven't studied religion to the extent that others have. I cannot quote verse and phrase from the Bible or other so-called holy books which were written by man.

I say my argument comes from using common sense. If an all-powerful God existed who loved mankind as the preacher and the bible thumpers say He does, why would He let innocent children die in the Holocausts? Why would He have let millions of Black people be taken off of the continent of Africa to be taken into slavery in the Americas? Why would He allow natural disasters, such as the Gujarat Earthquake in India in 2001, kill 20,000 people or the Black Death in Europe, from 1348-1351, to kill 75-200 million people? Mind you, I am not blaming those occurrences on God because there is no God. There are a lot of things that happen in this world that man does not have the answer for and that he cannot control. Man has formed the habit of saying that God is responsible for those happenings and that it is God's will that they happen. They give God credit for the good things that happen and the devil, who they say God created, gets credit for the terrible things that happen to man.

As time has progressed, man has increased his knowledge of the natural world. That increased knowledge has debunked man's prior explanations of everything from the reasons for natural disasters to the creation of man himself. In years past, earthquakes and epidemics were attributed by some, to the wrath of God—for God's displeasure about something or other that man did. Today, we understand that earthquakes are caused by the plate movement in the earth. Epidemics are caused by germs or viruses that we now have some control over. The discovery of one body of knowledge leads to more knowledge in the same or other areas.

The Christian religion long held on to the theory of the creation of the earth by a God. As a child, I learned in catechism that God created the earth and man in six days, and He rested on the seventh day of the week. This version of the creation of man was seriously taught in the religion that I was raised in (Catholicism).

Now, science tells us that that version of the earth's creation is a fairy tale. Explosions with other orbital bodies, millions of years ago, created the earth and the buildup of a habitable planet took other millions of years to bring about what is earth today. It is estimated that the earth is around 4.54 billion years old. The earliest man lived on the earth only about 66 million years ago. The earliest humans were not Adam and Eve.

Religion, seeing that the Bible version of the creation of the earth was in conflict with the more credible scientific version of creation, tried to modify the version that was once accepted by religious people. Religious people changed their creation story to bring it in line with the scientific version and to keep their six-day version intact.

In the scientific version of creation, the scientist divided the creation of the earth into periods which they called Eons. An Eon period lasted for millions of years. The scientists estimate that it took better than four Eons to complete the creation of the earth. Man came into existence on earth in the last eon, which was about 66 million years ago. The creation of the Earth and the development of Earth during the Eon periods looked as thus:

Earth's Geological Advancements[13]

1. Hadean Eon—4.5 Billion Years Ago

    The earth is formed out of debris around explosion of the solar system

2. Archean Eon—2.5-4 Billion Years Ago

    The first form of life emerges at the very beginning of this Eon. Earth's atmosphere is also formed of volcanic and

---

[13] The World Book Encyclopedia, Volume 6 (Field Enterprises)

greenhouse gases during this period, of the development of the earth

3. Proterozoic Eon—2.5 Billion-541 Million Years ago

    A more complex form of multicellular organisms and bacteria begin producing oxygen, plants, animals and fungi

4. Phanerozoic Eon—66 Million Years Ago-Present

    Complex life, including vertebrates, begins to dominate the earth. Oceans, Insects, and reptiles, the descendants of dinosaurs and modern animals, including humans, evolve during this period in the maturity of the earth

In light of the above scientific proof that the earth and man were created over a period of billions of years, some religious people have changed the religious story of the Earth's creation to try to bring the tale in line with the scientific version of creation. They have indicated that the six days referred to in the Bible were not literally six days as we know six days to be and were taught to believe. They now indicate that the six days in the Bible coincided with the different scientific Eons.

As the years go by, and more scientific knowledge is acquired, expect the religious spokespersons to change the story of how God interfaced with mankind. But there are men who are ingrained in the concept of God who will never give that concept up no matter what proof that scientists put on the table.

Conclusion

The ultimate proof of "Is there or isn't there a God?" will become known to all mankind at some point in our existence. The millions of people who populated the earth and have already died know the truth. It's unfortunate that not one could come back and tell us how death is. When we die, we will either wake up in another place doing something different then what we were doing while we were alive on earth or we will have no existence after death.

I wish that I could envision that for those people who had a horrible life—those people who were murdered, starved to death, died in natural disasters, killed in wars, died in an accident, or experienced horrific lives in any way—a life after death that would compensate for the bad break in life they received while living. It would be great if those people could live out an eternity that made up for the suffering they experienced while they were living. I would wish that their afterlife would be bliss.

But there I go, doing what man has done since his existence. In the above, I was being creative and using my imagination to try and compensate for the people who have had bad luck in life. Religious people have done that throughout man's existence. They have been successful in selling the concept of a god and an afterlife to the multitude of people on the earth, no matter what religious faith one espouses to.

I have made my argument against there being a god. One thing I know for certain, we all will die and when we pass away from this life, we will either wake up to a new existence or we will have no existence after this life is over.

www.ingramcontent.com/pod-product-compliance
Lightning Source LLC
Chambersburg PA
CBHW071639050426
42443CB00026B/770